CW00327439

NUTCASES

TORT

AUSTRALIA
LBC Information Services
Sydney

CANADA and USA
Carswell
Toronto · Ontario

NEW ZEALAND
Brooker's
Auckland

SINGAPORE and MALAYSIA
Sweet & Maxwell Asia
Singapore and Kuala Lumpur

NUTCASES

TORT

SECOND EDITION

by

VERA BERMINGHAM, M.A.
Senior Lecturer in Law
Kingston University

London · Hong Kong · Dublin
Sweet & Maxwell
1999

Published in 1999 by
Sweet & Maxwell Limited
of 100 Avenue Road
London, NW3 3PF
http://www.sweetandmaxwell.co.uk

Reprinted 2000, 2001

Computerset by J&L Composition Ltd, Filey, North Yorkshire
Printed in Italy by Legoprint S.p.A. Lavis, Trento

No natural forests were destroyed to make this product:
only farmed timber was used and re-planted

A CIP catalogue record for this book is available
from the British Library

ISBN 0–421–65290X

CONTENTS

TABLE OF CASES

TABLE OF STATUTES

1. TRESPASS TO PERSON

The Distinction Between Trespass and Negligence

Key Principle: **In addition to the act of interference, trespass requires proof of either intention or negligence.**

Stanley v. Powell 1891
The defendant had inflicted the injury neither intentionally nor negligently when he fired a shot which ricocheted off a tree and hit the plaintiff.

HELD: In confirming that trespass is a fault based tort, Denman J. further held that the burden of proof in negligence was on the plaintiff but in trespass the burden of disproving fault was on the defendant. [1891] 1 Q.B. 86

COMMENTARY
Whether there could be liability in trespass in the absence of negligence is a matter of some historical dispute. However, this case was interpreted to mean that if the defendant could show that s/he had not been negligent the plaintiff's claim would fail.

Key Principle: **In trespass to the person the burden of proving negligence lies on the plaintiff.**

Fowler v. Lanning 1959
Neither intention nor negligence was alleged by the plaintiff who was injured by a shot from the defendants gun. He argued that in trespass the burden of disproving negligence lay on the plaintiff and his statement of claim merely recorded "the defendant shot the plaintiff".

HELD: Since the claim lacked an allegation of intention or negligence, it was struck out as disclosing no cause of action. In this decision Diplock J. removed the supposed advantage of a trespass action, namely that the burden of disproving fault lay with the defendant. [1959] 1 Q.B. 426

Key Principle: Today, the general principle is that direct intentional acts of interference are dealt with by the tort of trespass. Where acts are unintentional and indirect the action lies in negligence.

Letang v. Cooper 1965

The defendant negligently drove his car over the legs of the plaintiff who was sunbathing on an hotel car park. More than three years later the plaintiff sued the defendant. Personal injury actions for "negligence, nuisance or breach of duty" must be brought within three years under the Limitation Act 1980, but other tort actions are barred only after six years. The plaintiff relied on trespass in an effort to prevent her action from being statute barred.

HELD: (CA) Lord Denning, with whom Danckwerths L.J. agreed, held that actions for personal injuries should no longer be divided into trespass (where the harm is direct) and case (for indirect harm) but according to nature of the defendant's conduct. If the conduct was intentional it was trespass. Where the conduct was negligent, the case of action is in negligence and not trespass. [1965] 1 Q.B. 232

COMMENTARY

The views of Lord Denning and Danckwerths L.J. that where the contact between the plaintiff and defendant was unintentional the claim must be brought in negligence, was approved by the Court of Appeal in *Wilson v. Pringle* [1987] (see p. 4). Note also, Lord Denning's argument that the phrase "breach of duty" in the Limitation Act 1980 covered any tort, including trespass, has been decisively rejected by the House of Lords in *Stubbings v. Webb* [1993] 1 All E.R. 322.

Assault and Battery

Assault

Key Principle: An assault requires no physical contact, it is essentially conduct which causes the reasonable apprehension of an immediate battery.

Stephens v. Myers 1830

The plaintiff was chairman of a parish meeting at which it was resolved, by a large majority, to expel the defendant. The defendant became vociferous and advanced towards the plaintiff saying that he would rather pull him out of the chair than be ejected. As he moved to unseat the plaintiff he was prevented by the church-warden from doing so.

HELD: The threat was sufficient to put the plaintiff in reasonable apprehension of an immediate battery. Lord Tindal C.J. stated that "though he was not near enough at the time to have struck him, yet if he was advancing with intent, I think it amounts to an assault in law." [1830] 4 C. & P. 349

Key Principle: Where the plaintiff has no reasonable belief that the defendant has the intention or the ability to carry out the threat immediately, no assault is committed.

Tuberville v. Savage 1669
The defendant placed his hand on his sword and said: "If it were not Assize time, I would not take such language from you."
HELD: By his own words the defendant had negated the possibility of a battery. (1669) 1 Mod. Rep. 3

COMMENTARY
This principle was applied in *Thomas v. National Union of Mineworkers* [1986] Ch. 20 where picketing miners made violent gestures at working miners who were being taken into the colliery in buses. It was held that there was no danger of an immediate battery since the working miners were safely in vehicles behind police barricades.

Battery

Key Principle: Battery is the actual infliction of unlawful force on another person. Any physical contact, no matter how trivial, is sufficient "force".

Collins v. Wilcock 1984
A woman police officer tried to question a woman whom she suspected of soliciting contrary to the Street Offences Act 1959. When she took hold of the woman's arm in order to detain her and administer a caution, the officer was not exercising a power of arrest.

HELD: The officer had gone beyond the scope of her duty in detaining the woman in circumstances short of arresting her and had therefore committed a battery. [1984] 3 All E.R. 374

COMMENTARY
Goff L.J. held the fundamental principle to be that every person's body is inviolate. However, he went on to state that bodily contact was not actionable if it was regarded as "falling within a general exception embracing all physical contact which is generally acceptable in the ordinary conduct of daily life."

Key Principle: **Unless it is self evident from the act itself, the defendant must show the contact to be hostile.**

Wilson v. Pringle 1987
The defendant schoolboy admitted that as an act of ordinary horseplay in a school corridor he pulled the plaintiff's schoolbag from his shoulder. This caused the plaintiff to fall and suffer a hip injury and he applied for a summary judgment on the ground that the defendant's admission amounted to a clear case of battery to which there was no defence. The trial judge accepted this view and the defendant appealed.
HELD: (CA) The trial judge had been wrong to grant summary judgment. Croom-Johnson L.J. stated that "in battery there must be an intentional touching or contact in one form or another of the plaintiff by the defendant. That touching must be proved to be a hostile touching." [1987] Q.B. 237

COMMENTARY
(1) This decision has been criticised for failing to define what is meant by "hostile". The court gave a number of examples of what is not hostile, but only one example of what it is, but it seems to mean little more than that the defendant wilfully interferes with the plaintiff in a way to which s/he is known to object. The test has not been well received in the House of Lords, in *Re F* [1990] 2 A.C. 1, Lord Goff doubted whether it is correct to say that the touching must be hostile for the purpose of battery. He stated that "A prank that gets out of hand, an over friendly slap on the back, surgical treatment by a surgeon who mistakenly thinks that the patient has consented to it, all these things may

transcend the bound of lawfulness, without being characterised as hostile. Indeed, the suggested qualification is difficult to reconcile with the principle that any touching of another's body is, in the absence of lawful excuse, capable of amounting to a battery and a trespass."

(2) The intention required in battery is that the defendant must have intended to commit the act that constitutes the trespass. An intention to hurt the plaintiff is not necessary. For example, in *Nash v. Sheehan*, the defendant hairdresser was liable in battery when a tone rinse was given to a plaintiff who had requested a permanent wave. In *Livingstone v. Ministry of Defence* [1984] N.I. 356 the defendant, a soldier, intended to hit someone other than the victim. He was found liable in battery when he fired a baton round at a rioter but missed and struck the plaintiff.

(3) As well as bodily integrity, the tort of battery protects the plaintiff's dignity. An action can be brought where there is indignity but no physical injury or where the plaintiff's rights have been infringed, for example, in relation to unlawful fingerprinting. In these cases, the plaintiff may only want to establish a principle, rather than to seek compensation and will therefore sue in trespass rather than negligence. Trespass is actionable *per se* (it is not necessary to prove damage) but in order to succeed in negligence the plaintiff must prove damage.

Key Principle: **Where there is no contact or physical force used, liability can arise for any intentionally inflicted bodily harm.**

Wilkinson v. Downton 1897

The defendant, as a practical joke, told the plaintiff that her husband had been seriously injured in an accident. As a result the plaintiff suffered a severe nervous disorder but the specific requirements of assault and battery—the application, or threat, of force—were not present.

HELD: Where an act wilfully calculated to cause physical damage, actually does cause such harm, there will be liability in trespass. It should be noted that at this time there was no liability in negligence for nervous shock. [1897] 2 Q.B. 57

COMMENTARY

(1) In *Khorasandjian v. Bush* [1993] 3 All E.R. 669, a case involving intentional harassment by telephone calls, the

Court of Appeal extended the principle in *Wilkinson v. Downton*. The plaintiff succeeded because there was a risk that the cumulative effect of the unrestrained telephone calls would cause physical or psychiatric damage.

(2) Subsequently, in *Burris v. Azadani* [1995] 4 All E.R. 802, the Court of Appeal recognised harassment as a cause of action.

(3) In *Hunter v. Canary Wharf Ltd* [1997] (see p. 129) the House of Lords was prepared to preserve the rule in *Wilkinson v. Downton* as a general cause of action. However, it anticipated that plaintiffs in these cases ought to rely on new statutory provisions contained in the Protection from Harassment Act 1997 rather than on the common law. Nevertheless, in cases where there is a single act of harassment (which is not covered by the act) it may still be open to the plaintiff to rely on *Wilkinson v. Downton*.

(4) Harassment was not fully defined in the 1997 Act but in *Huntington Life Sciences v. Curtin and Others, The Times*, December 11, 1997, Eadie J. said that the Act was clearly not intended by Parliament to be used to clamp down on the discussion of matters of public interest or upon the rights of political protest and public demonstration.

False Imprisonment

Key Principle: **False imprisonment does not require incarceration or the use of force but the unlawful constraint on another's freedom of movement must be total.**

Bird v. Jones 1845

The defendants, in order to provide seating for spectators at a regatta, wrongfully cordoned off a footpath on Hammersmith bridge. The plaintiff insisted on his right to use a part of the highway that had been cordoned off. He was prevented from doing so by the defendant and was told that he could go back the way he had come. [1845] 7 Q.B. 742

HELD: This was not false imprisonment. Since the plaintiff had a way out and decided not to take it there was no total restraint on his liberty.

COMMENTARY

In *R. v. Bournewood Community and Mental NHS Trust* [1998] 3 All E.R. 289, a majority of the House of Lords held that a patient in an open, unlocked ward was not in fact detained. This was the case notwithstanding the fact that if the patient had attempted to leave the medical staff would have prevented him from doing so by detaining him compulsorily under the Mental Health Act 1983.

Key Principle: **Where the plaintiff consents to the confinement there is no false imprisonment.**

Herd v. Weardale Steel, Coal and Coke Co. 1915

The plaintiff, a miner, refused to carry out what he believed to be dangerous work and demanded to be brought up to the mine surface. The employer refused to authorise the lift to be operated until the scheduled time at the end of the shift.

HELD: (HL) This was not false imprisonment because the plaintiff had voluntarily descended into the mine. [1915] A.C. 67

COMMENTARY

An alternative explanation for this decision is that there was no positive act to restrain the plaintiff and trespass does not lie for a mere omission.

Key Principle: **Where a plaintiff's liberty is subject to a reasonable condition it is not false imprisonment to restrain the plaintiff until that condition is fulfilled.**

Robinson v. Balmain Ferry Co. Ltd 1910

The plaintiff (a lawyer) decided that he could not wait 20 minutes for a ferry and decided to leave the wharf. When he refused to pay the one penny exit charge at the turnstile the defendant's employee refused to let him through.

HELD: (PC) There was no imprisonment because the condition of paying a penny to leave was a reasonable one in the circumstances. [1910] A.C. 295

Key Principle: Knowledge of the restraint at the time is not necessary to succeed in an action for false imprisonment.

Meering v. Graheme-White Aviation Co. Ltd (1920)
The plaintiff was suspected of theft from his employers. He was taken by two of the works police to the company's office for questioning. Unknown to the plaintiff, the police waited outside the office and, if the plaintiff had tried to leave, they would have prevented him from doing so.
HELD: (CA) Atkin L.J. said that there was no need for the plaintiff to have been aware of the imprisonment. However, knowledge of the detention might be relevant to the assessment of damages. [1919] 122 L.T. 44

COMMENTARY
(1) In this case the court failed to consider an earlier decision, *Herring v. Boyle* (1834) 1 Cr. M. & R. 377, where, because of unpaid school fees, the headmaster refused to allow a mother to take her son home for the Christmas holidays. It was held that, since the boy was unaware of the detention, there was no false imprisonment. However, the conflict of authority was resolved in Murray v. Ministry of Defence [1988] 1 W.L.R. 692, where the House of Lords disapproved of Herring and approved Meering.
(2) In *R. v. Bournewood Community and Mental NHS Trust* [1998] (p. 6) the House of Lords held that although in cases of false imprisonment it is not necessary for the plaintiff to be aware of the detention, there must be an *actual* rather than a potential restraint on the plaintiff's liberty.

Defences to Trespass to the Person

A number of statutes authorise conduct that would, under different conditions, amount to trespass to the person: the Police and Criminal Evidence Act 1984 provides police with a defence to what might otherwise constitute false imprisonment or battery; the Mental Health Act 1983 makes provision for the compulsory admission to hospital and treatment in relation to mental health; under the Children and Young Persons Act 1933 parents can justify an assault and battery by way of chastisement of their children. Disciplinary powers also remain for the captain of a ship: reasonable force may be exercised to preserve discipline for the safety of the ship, its crew, passengers and cargo, *Hook v. Cunard Steamship Co.* [1953] 1 W.L.R. 682.

Self-defence

Key Principle: **Self-defence will be a justification to an action in battery if the force used is reasonable.**

Cockroft v. Smith 1705
The plaintiff, Cockroft, was the clerk of the court. During a scuffle in court he ran his forefinger towards Smith's eyes. He sued Smith, who bit off his finger during the incident, and the question was whether self-defence was a proper defence. 11 Mod. 43

HELD:

(1) A person may use reasonable force in self-defence. Holt L.J., said ". . . hitting a man a little blow with a little stick on the shoulder, is not a reason for him to draw a sword and cut and hew the other . . .".
(2) See also *Revill v. Newbury* (1996) (see p. 121).

COMMENTARY
Force may be used defensively under the Criminal Law Act 1967, section 3 provides that "a person may use such force as is reasonable in the circumstances in the prevention of crime . . ."

Necessity

Key Principle: **The defence of necessity to trespass to the person may be invoked where the defendant acts for the purpose of protecting the plaintiff's own health or safety.**

Leigh v. Gladstone 1909
The plaintiff, a suffragette prisoner on hunger strike was forcibly fed by prison staff. When she claimed damages for trespass the defence was that that the acts were necessary to save her life and that the force used was the minimum necessary.
HELD: Her action failed because the court held that it was lawful for prison officials to intervene because they had a duty to preserve the life and health of those in their custody. (1909) 26 T.L.R. 130

COMMENTARY

(1) However, in Airedale in *Airedale NHS Trust v. Bland* [1993] 1 E.R. 821, the House of Lords held that an adult patient has the absolute right to refuse to consent to treatment, even if the consequence is that s/he will suffer serious injury or die. Lord Keith commented that the principle of sanctity of life is not an absolute one. It does not authorise force feeding of prisoners.

(2) In *R. v. Bournewood Community and Mental Health NHS Trust* (see p. 6) the House of Lords applied the principle of necessity and confirmed that the test of what is necessary is the "best interests of the patient" and this is to be determined by the *Bolam* test (see p. 41).

Key Principle: **Where an adult permanently lacks the mental capacity to give a valid consent the defence of necessity, provided it is in the best interests of the patient, will protect a doctor who gives medical treatment**

F v. West Berkshire Health Authority 1990

F, a 36 year old woman was said to have the mental capacity of a child about the age of five. She was cared for as a voluntary patient in a mental hospital and was thought by staff to have started a full sexual relationship with a male patient from the same hospital. It was proposed that she be sterilised and her mother applied to the court for a declaration that the operation would not be unlawful. **HELD:** (HL) The operation would be lawful. Lord Goff stated that the doctor must act in the best interests of the patient and ". . . in accordance with a responsible and competent body of relevant professional opinion . . . " *Bolam* test (see p. 41) [1990] 2 A.C. 1

COMMENTARY

(1) Although Lord Goff said that any medical treatment of a competent adult patient will be unlawful unless the patient has consented to the treatment, in *Re S* [1992] 4 All E.R. 671 the court declared it lawful to perform an operation on a competent pregnant woman who refused consent (on religious grounds) to a Cesarean section. The doctors were clear that the child could not survive without the operation and necessity was invoked in the vital interests of the patient and to protect the unborn child. However, in *Re MB (Medical*

Treatment (1997) 8 Med. L.R. 217, CA, where the Court of Appeal had to decide whether to grant a declaration over-riding a patient's refusal to consent to a Caesarian section, it was stated that *Re S* was out of line with other authorities. The court restated the principle that a mentally competent patient had an absolute right to refuse to consent to medical treatment for any reason, rational or irrational, even where that reason might lead to his or her death. It was also confirmed that the only situation in which it was lawful for doctors to intervene was if the patient lacked the capacity to decide and the treatment was in the patient's best interests. In *Re MB* the Court of Appeal authorised the surgical inter-vention on the basis that the patient's needle phobia put her in a state of such panic that she lacked the capacity to decide. (2) *St George's Healthcare Trust v. S* [1998] 3 All E.R. 673, involved a case where a pregnant mother rejected medical advice as to treatment necessary to protect her and her unborn child. The Court of Appeal held that there was no authority to detain a patient under the Mental Health Act 1983 in order to perform a non-consensual Caesarian section.

Consent

Key Principle: **There is implied consent to physical contact that occurs within the ordinary conduct of a game or sport.**

R. v. Billinghurst 1978

In the course of a rugby game the plaintiff, who did not have the ball at the time, was deliberately punched in the face by an opponent.

HELD: There was a battery. Even though players are deemed to consent to force: "of a kind which could reasonably be expected to happen during a game" this does not include foul play that goes beyond what a reasonable participant would expect. Crim. L.R. 553

COMMENTARY

(1) In *Condon v. Basi* [1985] 2 All E.R. 453, the plaintiff suffered a broken leg as the result of a foul tackle in the course of a game of football. It was held that consent to reasonable contact is consent only to non-negligent behaviour and the defendant was found liable in negligence.

(2) There will be a trespass if there is a deviation from the procedure consented to. In *Nash v. Sheehan* [1953] C.L.R. 3726 the application of a tone rinse to a plaintiff who requested a permanent wave was held to be trespass.

Key Principle: **Participants who voluntarily involve themselves in fights are taken to have consented to the battery.**

Lane v. Holloway 1968
The plaintiff, a retired gardener aged 64, came back from the pub one night and provoked an argument by calling the defendant's wife "a monkey faced tart". The 23-year-old defendant struck the plaintiff a violent blow in the eye and inflicted a wound that needed 19 stitches.
HELD: There is no action in battery available to those who take part in fights, especially, "an ordinary fight with fists" because they would be taken to have consented to the battery. However, consent did not apply in this case because the plaintiff's conduct was trivial and the defendant gave a "savage blow out of all proportion to the occasion". [1968] 1 Q.B. 379

COMMENTARY
In *Barnes v. Nayer*, *The Times*, December 19, 1986, provocation was again involved when the defendant killed the plaintiff's wife with a machete after he and his family were subjected to a prolonged course of abuse by their neighbours. The Court of Appeal held that contributory negligence, *volenti* and *ex turpi causa* (see Chap. 6) could be a defence to trespass to the person. (The defences did not apply in this case because of the disparity between the deceased's acts and the defendant's deadly attack.)

Key Principle: **Medical treatment involving the direct application of force administered without the patient's consent, or giving treatment different to that for which consent has been given, constitutes a battery.**

Chatterton v. Gerson 1981
The plaintiff was suffering from severe pain caused by a trapped nerve for which the defendant, a specialist in the treatment of

chronic intractable pain, gave her spinal injections. This helped the pain for a while but it rendered her right leg numb. She claimed in trespass on the ground that her consent to the injection was invalid as she had not been warned of the risk or informed of the potential consequences.

HELD: The defendant was not liable in trespass. Where a patient is informed in broad terms of the nature of the procedure and consent is obtained failure to disclose the associated risks does not invalidate the consent. [1981] Q.B. 432

COMMENTARY
Any action in respect of a doctor's failure to disclose sufficiently the risks inherent in medical treatment must be based in negligence. (See *Sidaway v. Bethlem Royal Hospital Governors*.)

2. VICARIOUS LIABILITY

Before vicarious liability is imposed on a defendant there are two conditions which must be met. First, there must be a specific employer-employee relationship. This is distinguished from an employer's relationship with a self employed independent contractor: employers are not usually liable for the torts of independent contractors. It can sometimes be difficult to define the status of an employment relationship, for example in the case of casual workers or where the working relationship does not fall into a traditional pattern. One accepted distinction is that those working under "a contract of service" are employees and those working under "contract for services" are independent contractors. A further test which produces straightforward answers in some cases is that of control: the crucial factor being the degree of control exercised by the employer over the way in which the work is done. But in modern working conditions the control test is not sufficient. There are many contracts of service where the employer does not or cannot control the way in which the work is done, for example, a surgeon working for the

National Health Service would not fit the control test. Therefore, the emphasis on the control test has been reduced and instead of relying on a single test the courts now consider a wide range of factors in each particular case. The second condition which must exist before an employer will be held liable for an employee's tort is that it must be committed when the employee is acting in the course of employment.

Key Principle: **The express intentions of the parties as to the classification of their working relationship is an important factor, but it is not conclusive.**

Ferguson v. John Dawson & Partners (Contractors) Ltd 1976
The plaintiff, a building worker, was injured when he fell off a roof at the defendant's construction site. Contrary to regulations there was no guard rail on the roof. If he had been an independent contractor he would have been responsible for his own safety and unable to sue the company. At the time of hiring the plaintiff was expressed to be a "labour only sub-contractor" although he was an unskilled labourer and subject to the control of the site agent. **HELD:** (CA) The employers were liable. Despite the label that the parties had given to the relationship, in all other respects the plaintiff was treated as an employee working under a contract for service. [1976] 1 W.L.R. 346

COMMENTARY
(1) In *Ready Mixed Concrete (S.E.) Ltd v. Minister of Pensions* (1968) (see below) it was held that where the parties have specified that a person will be self-employed, and the other terms of the contract do not show otherwise, the contract will be regarded as a contract for services.
(2) In *Stevenson, Jordan & Harrison Ltd v. Macdonald & Evans* (1952) 1 T.L.R. 101, the "integration test" was proposed by Lord Denning: an employee is someone whose work is an integral part of the business; an independent contractor is someone who would work for the business, but as an accessory rather than an integral part of it. This test has been applied in some situations but it has failed as a universal test and the courts have now moved to a multiple approach.

Key Principle: In determining the nature of the employment relationship there are a number of relevant factors to be considered. The allocation of financial risk is one of these factors and this particular question should be addressed by asking: Is the person in business on his or her own behalf?

Ready-Mixed Concrete (S.E.) Ltd v. Minister of Pensions 1968
A concrete-manufacturing company introduced a scheme whereby its concrete would be transported by a team of "owner-drivers" who would be paid a fixed mileage rate for the service. The plaintiff driver's contract described him as an independent contractor, and he was obliged to maintain his vehicle in good order at his own expense. He had no fixed hours of work and could choose his own routes and he was also free to employ a competent driver when necessary. However, he undertook to make his lorry available whenever the company wanted it, to have it painted the company's colours, and to wear the company uniform. The issue was whether the owner-drivers were employees of the company: if so, the company was liable to pay national insurance contributions in respect of them.
HELD: The driver was working under a contract for services. He owned the lorry, bore the financial risk and was, in fact, running his own business. [1968] 2 Q.B. 497

_____

Key Principle: Where an employee is lent out to another employer on a temporary basis the presumption is that the general (or original) employer remains vicariously liable.

Mersey Docks and Harbour Board v. Coggins and Griffith (Liverpool) Ltd 1947
A mobile crane and a driver had been hired out to a firm of stevedores under a contract which stipulated that the driver was to be the employee of the stevedores. In spite of this term his original employer, the Board, paid his wages and retained the right to dismiss him. The hirer directed the tasks which were to be performed by the driver but not how he was to operate the crane. In the course of his work the driver negligently injured the plaintiff and the question to be determined was whether the stevedores or the Board were vicariously liable.
HELD: (HL) Several factors have to be considered but the decisive question to be asked was who bore the ultimate control over

the manner in which the work was performed. On the facts of the case the Board remained liable. [1947] A.C. 1

COMMENTARY

(1) The burden of proof remains with the original employer to show that responsibility for the torts of the employee has shifted to the second employer.

(2) It was also held that an express term in the contract of hire stating that the workman is the employee of the hirer is not to be treated as conclusive.

Course of Employment

Key Principle: **Where an act which is authorised by an employer is performed by the employee in a wrongful and unauthorised manner, the employer remains liable.**

Whatman v. Pearson 1868

The employees were allowed an hour for dinner but were forbidden to go home, or to leave their horses and carts unguarded. However, one of the employees went home for dinner anyway, making a deviation in his route of about a quarter of a mile. When he negligently left his horse out in the street it bolted and damaged the plaintiff's property.

HELD: The employee's duties involved looking after the horse and cart all day and he was therefore acting within the scope of his employment. (1868) L.R. 3 C.P. 422

Key Principle: **A new and separate journey will take the employee outside the course of employment.**

Storey v. Ashton 1869

The employees were instructed to deliver some wine and on the return journey one of the employees persuaded the other, that since it was by then after hours, to set off in a different direction to visit some relatives. On the way there the plaintiff was injured by the employee's negligent driving.

HELD: The driver was not acting in the course of employment, it was a new and independent journey which was entirely for his own business. (1869) L.R. 4 Q.B. 476

COMMENTARY
(1) This corresponds with *Joel v. Morrison* (1834) 6 C. & P. 501 where the test was said to be whether the employee was engaged on the employer's business or "on a frolic of his own".
(2) Cockburn C.J. said it was a question of degree how far a deviation from the authorised route would be considered a separate journey.
(3) In *Harvey v. R.G. O'Dell Ltd* [1958] 2 Q.B. 78, a five-mile journey to get a midday meal during working hours was held to be within the course of employment.

Key Principle: An employee travelling between home and work will not generally be in the course of employment. But an employee travelling *in the employer's time* from home to a workplace other than the regular workplace or between workplaces will be within the course of employment.

Smith v. Stages 1989
A peripatetic lagger was working at a power station in the midlands when his employer sent him and another employee to perform an urgent job in Wales. In addition to their hourly rate they were paid travelling expenses for the journeys there and back. They were using a private vehicle and had discretion as to how and when they would travel. Having worked without sleep they finished the job two days early and decided to drive straight home. As they were travelling back together in the car they were both injured when the employee driving the car crashed into a wall. The driver was uninsured and the plaintiff sued the employer on the basis of vicarious liability.
HELD: (HL) The employers were liable. Lord Goff said the fact that the men were travelling back early was immaterial since they were still being paid wages to travel there and back. Lord Lowry thought the crucial point was that the employees were "on duty" at the time of the accident. [1989] A.C. 928

Key Principle: **An act may be within the course of employment even though it has been expressly forbidden by the employer.**

Limpus v. London General Omnibus Co. 1862
A bus driver was instructed not to race with or obstruct the buses of rival companies. He disobeyed this instruction and caused an accident in which the plaintiff's horses were injured.
HELD: Despite the prohibition the employers were liable since this was simply an improper method adopted by the employee in performing his duties. (1862) 1 H. & C. 526

COMMENTARY
It is outside the course of employment for an employee to do something which is not connected with what s/he is employed to do. In *Beard v. London General Omnibus Co.* [1900] 2 Q.B. 530, a bus conductor, in the driver's absence, decided to turn the bus around for the return journey. As a conductor, it was not his job to drive the bus and he was therefore acting outside the course of his employment.

Key Principle: **Where a prohibited act is performed in furthering the employer's business it is usually within the course of employment.**

Rose v. Plenty 1976
A milkman employed a boy aged 13 to help him on his milk round despite his employer's express instruction not to do so. Due mainly to the milkman's negligent driving the boy was injured.
HELD: (CA) The employers were liable. Lord Denning said the driver was still within the course of employment despite the express prohibition because he was still acting for the master's purposes, business, and benefit. [1976] 1 W.L.R. 141

COMMENTARY
In *Conway v. George Wimpey & Co.* [1951] 2 K.B. 266 a lorry driver, contrary to express instructions, who gave a lift to an employee of another firm of contractors was acting outside the course of his employment. Apart from the fact that the driver was held to be performing an act which he was not employed to perform at all, the unauthorised passenger must have known from the notices inside the vehicle that he was a trespasser.

Key Principle: When considering the scope of employment it is enough to show that the employee was generally doing his job at the time, and doing a job negligently does not take an employee outside the course of employment.

Century Insurance Co. Ltd v. Northern Ireland Road Transport Board 1942
The driver of a petrol lorry was transferring petrol from the lorry into a tank at a garage. He lit a cigarette and negligently threw down a lighted match. This caused an explosion and fire.
HELD: (HL) The defendants were liable. At the time of the act, even though the employee was plainly negligent, he was delivering petrol. This was the very purpose for which he was employed. [1942] A.C. 509

Key Principle: Where a deliberate assault is involved the courts are reluctant to find that the employee was acting in the course of employment.

Warren v. Henlys 1948
An employee engaged as petrol pump attendant by the defendant mistakenly thought that the plaintiff was attempting to drive away without paying for some petrol. He made this accusation to the plaintiff in violent language. The plaintiff paid his bill, called the police and when he threatened to report the pump attendant to his employers he was assaulted and injured by him. The plaintiff brought an action against the employers.
HELD: The defendants were not liable, the assault was a mere act of personal vengeance and outside the course of employment. [1948] 2 All E.R. 935

COMMENTARY
Similarly in *Keppel Bus Co. Ltd v. Sa'ad bin Ahmad* [1974] W.L.R. 1082 a passenger was not allowed to recover when a bus conductor blinded him with his ticket punch.

Key Principle: There are occasions when an employer will be vicariously responsible for deliberate criminal conduct of an employee.

Lloyd v. Grace Smith & Co. 1912
The defendants, a firm of solicitors, employed a clerk who fraudulently induced a client into transferring some cottages over to him. He then dishonestly disposed of the property and stole the proceeds.
HELD: (HL) Even though the fraud was not committed for the benefit of the employers and they were ignorant of his schemes they were liable because they had held the clerk out as having authority to perform the type of transaction in question. [1912] A.C.716

COMMENTARY
(1) Similarly in *Morris v. Martin (C.W.) & Sons Ltd* [1996] 1 Q.B. 716, a firm of dry cleaners were found liable by the Court of Appeal when the plaintiff's fur coat was stolen by an employee.
(2) In *Generale Bank Nederland NV v. Export Credits Guarantee Department*, *The Times*, February 18, 1999, the plaintiff claimed that the defendants were liable because one of their employees had assisted in a fraudster's deceit by underwriting guarantees. The House of Lords upheld the Court of Appeal decision that an employer had no liability in tort for his employee's acts, done in the course of employment to assist in the fraudulent scheme of a third person, unless the acts were within the employee's actual or ostensible authority. The mere fact that his employment provided the employee with the opportunity to facilitate fraud was not sufficient to render an employer vicariously liable.

Employer's Indemnity

Key Principle: An employer who has been held vicariously liable for an employee's negligence is entitled to seek an indemnity from the employee to recover any damages paid.

Lister v. Romford Ice & Cold Storage Co. 1957
Lister was employed as a lorry driver. In the course of his employment he was driving negligently when he injured his father, a fellow employee. The employers were vicariously liable and the

father's damages were paid by the employers' insurers. Exercising their right of subrogation the insurers then brought an action against the son for an indemnity.
HELD: (HL) The son was liable to indemnify the employers, and hence the insurers. [1957] A.C. 555

COMMENTARY
(1) It must be noted that the employer is liable as well as the employee. As joint tort-feasors they are each fully liable to the plaintiff.
(2) Because of the problems predicted for industrial relations following this decision the employers' liability insurers entered into a "gentleman's agreement" not to take advantage of this principle unless there was evidence of collusion or misconduct.

Employer's Liability for Independent Contractors

Key Principle: Although employers are *not generally* liable for their contractor's torts, an employer will be responsible for the acts of independent contractors who carry out extra hazardous activities. Where the task is inherently dangerous the duty on an employer is so onerous that it cannot be delegated to anyone else.

Honeywell and Stein Ltd v. Larkin Bros Ltd 1934
The plaintiffs did some work in a cinema and, having obtained the permission of the cinema owners, engaged the defendants as independent contractors to take photographs of their work. In those days this task involved igniting magnesium powder and in doing so the defendant's employee negligently set the curtains on fire. The plaintiffs paid the cinema owners for the damage caused by the fire and sought to recover from the defendants.
HELD: (CA) The plaintiffs had remained liable for the damage caused by the independent contractors because the task involved was extra hazardous. A duty is non-delegable where acts "in their very nature, involve . . . special danger to others". [1934] 1 K.B. 191

COMMENTARY
(1) A further exception to the rule that an employer is not liable for the torts of an independent contractor is where the work is carried out on or adjoining the highway. In *Tarry v.*

Ashton (1876) 1 Q.B.D. 314 the occupier of a public house adjoining the highway was liable when a heavy lamp attached to the building injured a passer–by. Although the occupier argued that he had employed an independent contractor to keep the lamp in good repair, it was held that the duty to maintain premises so close to the highway could not be delegated.

(2) In *Rowe v. Herman* [1997] 1 W.L.R. 1390, the Court of Appeal restated the basic principle that an employer is not liable for an independent contractor's negligence. In this case there was no question of works on the highway involving extra hazardous acts and, on the facts of the case, the defendant occupiers were not responsible for the negligence of an independent contractor working on their land.

(3) Note also that an employer's duty for the safety of employees is non-delegable. *Wilson v. Clyde Coal Co. Ltd* (see p. 82).

3. NEGLIGENCE: DUTY OF CARE

As a tort, negligence consists of three elements: a legal *duty* to take care; *breach* of that duty and *damage* suffered as a consequence of that breach. In this Chapter cases relating to the duty element will be outlined, Chapter four will then focus on cases concerning breach of duty and damage will be the subject of the cases in Chapter five. However, it might be useful at this point to note that these key concepts overalp and that the separate elements frequently fail to provide a clear answer as to whether a claim should be allowed. In *Lamb v. Camden LBC* (1981) Lord Denning said: "it is not every consequence of a wrongful act which is the subject of compensation". Lines have to be drawn somewhere:

"Sometimes it is done by limiting the range of persons to whom a duty is owed. Sometimes it is done by saying that there is a break in the chain of causation. At other times it is done by saying that the consequence is too remote to be a head of damage. All these devices are useful in their way. Ultimately, it is a question of policy for judges to decide".

In *Caparo Industries v. Dickman* (1990) (see p. 71) Lord Roskill commented that "it has now to be accepted that there is no simple formula or touchstone" in the formulation of the test for existence of a duty of care:

> "Phrases such as 'foreseeability', 'proximity', 'neighbourhood', 'just and reasonable' 'fairness', 'voluntary acceptance of risk' or 'voluntary assumption of responsibility' will be found used from time to time in the different cases. But . . . such phrases are not precise definitions. At best they are but labels or phrases descriptive of the very different factual situations which can exist in particular cases and which must be carefully examined in each case before it can be pragmatically determined whether a duty of care exists and, if so, what is the scope of that duty."

Key Principle: Negligence is an independent tort for which the existence of a *duty of care* is a prerequisite of liability.

Donoghue v. Stevenson 1932

The plaintiff went to a café with a friend who ordered some drinks. When the drinks arrived the plaintiff drank some of the contents and she alleged that when her friend poured the remainder of the drink into her glass it contained the remnants of a decomposed snail. As a result she became seriously ill. She could not sue the retailer with whom she had no contract nor could she plausibly claim that he was negligent because the bottle was opaque and the snail could not be seen. Instead she sued the manufacturers of the drink in negligence. The manufacturers raised the defence of privity and claimed that since the plaintiff could not sue them in contract she could not sue them in tort either.

HELD: (HL) There could be a remedy in tort—a manufacturer had a duty of care in negligence to the ultimate consumer of his products. According to Lord Atkin, "You must take reasonable care to avoid acts or omissions which you can reasonably foresee would be likely to injure your neighbour." "Neighbour", in the legal sense, he defined as "persons who are so closely and directly affected by my act that I ought reasonably to have them in contemplation as being so affected when I am directing my mind to the acts or omissions which are called in question." [1932] A.C. 562

COMMENTARY

(1) Liability for negligent conduct had previously been recognised only in certain carefully defined circumstances. The court allowed actions for damages in cases where the

special circumstances gave rise to a duty of care such as, for example, doctor-patient, innkeeper-guest, or where fire damage resulted from negligence. Lord Atkin sought to unify these disparate duties of care in a single general theory and stated that the courts had previously been "engaged upon an elaborate classification of duties as they existed in various fact situations. . .".

(2) In addition to the notion of foresight and reasonable contemplatin of harm, Lord Atkin emphasised the need for a relationship of *proximity* between the parties, but this does not necessarily mean that the plaintiff must be in a close physical or spatial relationship to the defendant. Discussion of the relationship of proximity can be found in the reasoning of many cases concerning the extent of liability for economic loss caused by negligent statements (For example, see *John Munroe*, p. 30.)

(3) In *Yeun Kun Yeu v. Attorney General of Hong Kong* (see p. 26) Lord Keith held the expression "proximity or neighbourhood" to be a composite one importing the whole concept of necessary relationship between the plaintiff and defendant.

(4) In *Hedley Byrne v. Heller* (1964) (see p. 67) the House of Lords confirmed the neighbour principle enunciated by Lord Atkin as a flexible test which could be applied in any fact situation. In *Home Office v. Dorset Yacht Co. Ltd* [1970] A.C. 1004, Lord Reid suggested that the neighbour principle based on reasonable foreseeability ought to apply in all cases unless some reason for its exclusion could be justified.

Key Principle: The test for the existence of a duty of care is to be approached in two stages.

Anns v. London Borough of Merton 1978

The plaintiffs were lessees of flats which they claimed suffered structural deterioration through being built on foundations of insufficient depth. They sued in negligence against the local authority on the basis that it had negligently failed to inspect the foundations or negligently carried out an inspection.

HELD: (HL) The local authority were liable: the exercise of statutory powers and statutory duties by public bodies could give rise to a duty of care to individuals. [1978] A.C. 728

COMMENTARY

In his speech Lord Wilberforce extended the neighbour principle based on reasonable foresight and introduced a two-stage test. In summary, this test is approached by asking the following two questions: first, was the harm foreseeable and thereby bringing the plaintiff within the neighbour principle? If so, then: was there any valid policy reason to deny the existence of a duty of care in this case? The first stage of Lord Wilberforce's test presented no hurdle to litigants at all and it appeared possible that the plaintiff, having established foreseeability of harm, raised the presumption of the existence of a duty of care. This meant that, at the second stage of the test (the policy stage) the courts were left to restrict the scope of negligence liability by reference to policy considerations.

Anns was seen as a liberating principle, for example in *McLaughlin v. O'Brian* (1983) (see p. 61) the policy arguments, which were said to justify the restrictions on liability, were criticised. Lord Bridge dismissing the floodgates argument said: "I believe that the floodgates argument . . . is, as it always has been, greatly exaggerated". This period of expansion of negligence liability reached its high-water mark in *Junior Books v. Veitchi Co. Ltd* (1983) (see p. 65). The House of Lords went one step further than *Anns* and allowed a claim in negligence where there was no allegation that the factory floor in question was dangerously defective—the defect in question was one of quality.

(2) In *Governors of the Peabody Donation Fund v. Sir Lindsay Parkinson & Co. Ltd* (1985) (see below) the House of Lords warned against the more liberal approach. Marking a retreat from *Anns*, in subsequent decisions the courts have sought to reassert limits on the scope of liability that had traditionally been recognised in the case law.

Key Principle: In the test for a duty of care it is now material to take into consideratin whether it is "just and reasonable" that a duty should be imposed.

Governors of the Peabody Donation Fund v. Sir Lindsay Parkinson & Co. Ltd 1985

The plaintiff development company was required by statute to provide an adequate drainage system for new dwellings under

construction. The drainage system, which had been approved by
the local authority, proved to be unsatisfactory and the plaintiff
suffered economic loss. The plaintiff alleged that the local authority had been in breach of its duty to ensure that the system was
suitable.

HELD: (HL) Lord Keith denied a remedy to the plaintiff. In
retreating from the *Wilberforce* two-stage test he introduced a
requirement that the plaintiff should identify policy grounds
why a duty should arise: why the defendant should be made
responsible for his welfare. He further stated:

> ". . . in determining whether or not a duty of care of particular scope
> was incumbent on a defendant it is material to take into consideration
> whether it is just and reasonable that it should be so . . ." [1985] A.C.
> 210

COMMENTARY
(1) Judicial criticism of *Anns* continued in *Yeun Kun Yei v.
Attorney General of Hong Kong* [1988] A.C. 175 where Lord
Keith said:

> "In view of the direction in which the law has since been developing,
> their Lordships consider that for the future it should be recognised that
> the two-stage test in *Anns* is not to be regarded as in all circumstances
> a suitable guide to the existence of a duty of care."

Key Principle: **A local authority is not liable in negligence to a
building owner or occupier for losses arising from its failure to
ensure that the building was designed or erected in accordance
with building regulations.**

Murphy v. Brentwood District Council 1990
The plaintiff had purchased a house which was constructed on a
concrete raft foundation over an in-filled site. In 1981 he discovered cracks in the house threatening the whole fabric of the
property. It was discovered that the concrete raft foundation had
subsided and the plaintiff sued the local council for negligently
approving plans for the foundations.

HELD: The local authority was not liable. The house had only
damaged itself and was therefore merely a defective house which
was a bad bargain: unless and until actual physical damage had

occurred the cost of making the house safe or any diminution in its value is purely economic loss. [1990] 1 A.C. 398

COMMENTARY

(1) A seven-member House of Lords found it necessary to overrule their own earlier decision in *Anns* (above). Of wider importance the case marks a contraction in the scope of a duty of care in economic loss cases. See also *D. & F. Estates Lrd v. Church Commissioners* (see p. 94).

(2) In *Caparo v. Dickman* (see p. 71) the House of Lords set down a tripartite test for establishing a duty of care: (i) the harm must have been reasonably foreseeable; (ii) there must have been a relationship of proximity between the parties; (iii) in all the circumstances of the case, it must be fair, just and reasonable to impose a duty of care. The Court approved *Sutherland Shire Council v. Heyman* [1985] 157 C.L.R. 424, in which Brennan J. rejected the broad principles approach taken by Lord Wilberforce in *Anns* and said that the law should develop "incrementally by analogy with established categories."

The Three Stage Approach

Key Principle: **Even if the requisite degree of proximity exists, a duty may still be denied if in the court's view the imposition of liability would not be fair just and reasonable. Whatever the nature of the harm suffered by the plaintiff, all three elements of the tripartite test, foreseeability, proximity and questions of justice and reasonableness, must be applied.**

Marc Rich & Co. v. Bishop Rock Marine Co. Ltd 1995

A vessel, "The Nicholas H", developed a crack while carrying a cargo from South America to Italy. A surveyor employed by a marine classification society pronounced that, with temporary welding work, the vessel was fit to complete the voyage. A few days later the ship sank with a total loss of the cargo.

HELD: (HL) The House of Lords held that the classification society owed no duty of care to the cargo owners. A number of policy factors pointed against a decision in favour of the owners. Classification societies were independent non-profit making entities, operating for the sole purpose of promoting the collective welfare, namely, the safety of ships and lives at sea. A finding of liability might lead to classification societies adopting a more "defensive position." If a duty of care was to be recognised it would enable cargo owners, or their insurers, to upset balance of the international conventions governing shopowners' liability to cargo owners. In addition, another layer of insurance cover wouuld be wastefully introduced into the structure. [1995] 3 All E.R. 307

COMMENTARY
In *Perrett v. Collins, The Times*, June 23, 1998, the Court of Appeal held that a certifying authority and its inspector who certified a light aircraft as fit to fly owed a duty of care to a passenger. The defendants sought to rely on *Marc Rich & Co.*, but the court held that the reasoning in *Marc Rich* was based upon broad policy considerations relating to the organisation of maritime trade which were peculiar to that situation. In the present case, the inspector had an independent and critical role in the granting of a certificate of fitness for flight, without which the aircraft could not take off.

Key Principle: The imposition of a duty of care in negligence upon a body exercising a public function could lead to that function being performed in a detrimentally defensive manner.

X v. Bedfordshire County Council 1995
Actions were taken against a number of local authorities. The cases against Bedfordshire and Newham concerned child abuse. It was alleged that the authorities had failed to diagnose abuse in one case, and in the other, had identified the wrong person as the abuser. In the cases involving Dorset, Bromley and Hampshire, it was alleged that the authorities had failed to properly identify and provide for the special educational needs of the plaintiffs.
HELD: (HL) The House of Lords ruled that it is not fair, just and reasonable to impose a duty on local authorities in discharging their function *vis-à-vis* the prevention of child abuse and the allocation of special schooling for those with learning difficulties. 1995 2 AC 633

COMMENTARY
(1) The Court of Appeal in *Phelps v. Hillingdon LBC, Lawtel*, November 4, 1998, allowed an appeal against a finding that an education psychologist, employed by the local authority, was under a duty of care to the plaintiff for failing to diagnose her dyslexia. Stuart Smith L.J. said that it was

most unsatisfactory that the local authority should be made liable by the back door of vicarious liability, unless that responsibility was clearly established.

(2) In *Barrett v. Enfield LBC* [1998] Q.B. 367 a foster child claimed that an authority was negligent in the way it made and supervised foster placements. The Court of Appeal held that it would not be fair just and reasonable to make a local authority directly liable for the way it made decisions about the bringing up of a child in care and said that the imposition of liability could lead to a defensive and cautious approach.

(3) In *Harris v. Evans* [1998] 3 All E.R. 522, similar reasoning was applied. The plaintiff started to offer bungee jumps from his mobile telescopic crane. The specialist inspector from the Health and Safety Executive advised that the plaintiff ought to take further measures to ensure the safety of participants and spectators and a prohibition notice was served on the plaintiff. When it subsequently became clear that the inspector's advice had been out of line with the Health and Safety Executive's policy the plaintiff sued for the economic losses that the had suffered as a result of the inspector's negligence. The Court of Appeal held that it was not fair, just and reasonable to impose a duty on the Health and Safety Executive. It was further held that the imposition of a duty of care would probably have a detrimental effect by producing an unduly cautious and defensive approach by inspectors.

Policy as a Criterion of Duty

Key Principle: **Public policy is capable of constituting a separate and independent ground for holding that liability in negligence should not be imposed.**

Hill v. Chief Constable of West Yorkshire 1988
The plaintiff was the mother of the last victim of the mass murderer the "Yorkshire Ripper". She claimed damages on the basis that the police had negligently failed to apprehend the murderer before her daughter was killed.

HELD: (HL) Notwithstanding that harm was reasonably foreseeable, there was insufficient proximity between the police and the victim. The House of Lords further stated that a general duty of care to protect all members of the public from the consequences of crime would be impracticable and, on grounds of public policy, deeply damaging to police operations. [1988] 2 All E.R. 238

COMMENTARY

(1) The public policy immunity granted in this case was extended beyond the failure of police to apprehend criminals in *Osman v. Ferguson* [1993] 4 All E.R. 344. There were fatal consequences when police had failed to act on warnings that a known individual was likely to commit serious offences. Although the Court of Appeal was prepared to accept that there was a sufficient relationship of proximity between the plaintiff's family and the police, the case nevertheless failed on grounds of public policy.

(2) In *John Munroe v. London Fire and Civil Defence Authority* [1997] 2 All E.R. 865, a number of consolidated appeals were heard in respect of claims in negligence against the fire brigade. The Court of Appeal confirmed the relevance of policy considerations including the possibility of defensive fire-fighting and held that there is no proximity of relationship between the fire brigade and a building owner in respect of negligence in the tackling of a fire. The fire brigade are not under a common law duty to answer a call for help, and unless the fire brigade actually increases the damage or causes additional damage there could be no liability. However, in *Kent v. Griffiths and Others, The Times*, December 23, 1998, the Court of Appeal held that although the ambulance service owed no duty to the public at large to respond to a call for help, once a 999 call in a serious emergency had been accepted, it was arguable that the ambulance service did have an obligation to provide the service for a named individual at a specified address.

(2) In *Swinney v. C.C. of Northumbria, The Times*, March 28, 1996, the Court of Appeal held that the immunity in respect of police activities in the investigation and suppression of crime could be displaced by other considerations of public policy for the protection of the public. The plaintiffs had given information to the police which could have helped to identify a hit and run driver. This information was given in confidence and when it was stolen from a police vehicle the plaintiffs suffered threats of violence. In spite of *Hill* the police were found not to have a blanket immunity and a duty of care was owed to the plaintiffs in the storage and safe keeping of the information.

(3) See also "wrongful life" and "wrongful birth" cases (p. 33).

(4) Public policy was considered in the context of redistribution of losses by Lord Denning in *Spartan Steel v. Martin & Co.* (1973) (sse p. 65)

Key Principle: Public policy requires that a barrister or a solicitor does not owe a duty of care to their client in respect of the manner in which a case is conducted in court.

Rondel v. Worsley 1969

The appellant was charged and convicted of grievous bodily harm. He was represented at the trial by the respondent barrister against whom he later issued a writ and statement of claim alleging negligence in the conduct of his defence. The legal point to be decided was whether such an action could lie.

HELD: (HL) A barrister is immune from liability in the conduct and management of a case in court on the public policy grounds that: (i) barristers should be able to carry out their duties independently and without fear; (ii) a barrister owes a duty to the court which transcends that owed to a client and potential liability might deflect from that duty; (iii) actions against barristers would in effect amount to a retrial in the cases where negligence was alleged; and (iv) under the "cab rank" rule of the Bar barristers are obliged to accept any client if a proper fee is paid. [1969] 1 A.C. 191

COMMENTARY

(1) In *Siaf Ali v. Sydney Mitchell & Co.* [1980] A.C. 198 this immunity was extended to pre-trial work which is intimately connected with the conduct of the case in court and under the Courts and Legal Services Act 1990, section 62(1), any person who is not a barrister but who lawfully provides any legal services in relation to proceedings shall have the same immunity.

(2) In *Elguzouli-Daf v. Metropolitan Police Commissioner* [1995] 2 W.L.R. 173 the Court of Appeal held that, in the absence of some voluntary assumption of responsibility to a particular defendant, the Crown Prosecution Service is immune from actions in negligence.

Liability for Acts of Third Parties

Key Principle: There is no general duty of care to prevent third parties from harming others by their deliberate wrongdoing.

Smith v. Littlewoods Organisation Ltd 1987

The defendants purchased a cinema which remained empty and unattended for over a month awaiting to be demolished and rebuilt as a supermarket. During this time it was regularly being broken into, mainly by children. Contractors employed by Littlewoods knew about the vandals but neither the defendant nor the police were informed about this. Finally, a fire was deliberately started by the vandals which spread and caused serious damage to the plaintiff's property. The plaintiffs claimed that the defendants should have prevented the vandals gaining access to the cinema.

HELD: (HL) The plaintiff's claim failed. Lord Goff dealt with the matter in terms of pure omission and held that there is no general duty of care to prevent a third party from causing damage. However, he expressed the view that liability would arise where "the defender negligently causes or permits to be created a source of danger, and it is reasonably foreseeable that third parties may interfere with it . . .". (see also breach of duty, p. 35) [1987] A.C. 1

COMMENTARY

In *Carmarthenshire* C.C. *v. Lewis* (see p. 44) where a local authority was held to have a duty to control the conduct of a child in order to prevent harm, the House of Lords confirmed the responsibility of parents and teachers for the behaviour of children.

Key Principle: Liability may arise in respect of the wrongdoing of others where the defendant is held to have undertaken a duty of care specifically to the plaintiff.

Stansbie v. Troman 1948

A decorator who was working in a house was warned by the householder to shut the front door if he left the premises. He carelessly left the house unlocked while he went to fetch more wallpaper. During his absence the house was burgled and some jewellery was stolen.

HELD: The decorator was liable for the loss of the jewellery stolen by a third party. His duty to the householder arose from an implied term in his employment contract to keep the premises safe. [1948] 2 K.B. 48

COMMENTARY

In *Topp v. London Country Bus (South West) Ltd* [1993] 1 W.L.R. 976, the Court of Appeal found no liability for the wrongdoing of a third party when a minibus which had been left parked with the key in the ignition was stolen by persons unknown. The plaintiff's wife was killed when the stolen minibus was being driven dangerously and he sued the defendant bus company. It was held that the parked minibus did not fall within a special category of risk as a source of danger on the highway and the acts of the wrongdoer were regarded as a *novus actus interveniens* (see p. 51)

Liability for the Unborn

Key Principle: A duty of care is owed to an unborn person which becomes actionable on the live birth of the child.

Burton v. Islington Health Authority 1993
The plaintiff's mother was admitted for an operation to the defendant hospital. At the time, unknown to the hospital, the woman was pregnant. The plaintiff alleged that she had been born with abnormalities because of the operation the defendants had performed on her mother when she was an embryo in her mother's womb. The defendants applied to strike out the claim on the ground that, at the time of the alleged negligence, the plaintiff had no legal status.
HELD: The plaintiff had a cause of action which is available to a child born alive for injuries sustained in the womb. [1993] Q.B. 204

COMMENTARY
The Congenital Disabilities (Civil Liability) Act 1976 was inapplicable in this case because the plaintiff was born before the Act came into force. The Act—which provids that a child who is born alive but disabled as a result of an occurrence before its birth may have a cause of action in negligence—has replaced the common law for births which occurred after July 22, 1976, the date upon which it came into force.

Key Principle: The common law recognises no claim for "wrongful life" whereby a child claims that s/he would not have been born at all, but for the defendant's negligence.

McKay v. Essex Area Health Authority 1982
The plaintiff's mother had undergone tests during her pregnancy when she realised that she had been in contact with rubella (German measles). The mother would have opted for an abortion had the tests proved positive but she had been negligently told that her

unborn child was not infected with rubella. The plaintiff was born with severe disabilities and claimed in respect of the harm caused to her by her birth encumbered by these disabilities.

HELD: (CA) The law recognised no claim for "wrongful life". To allow a child to recover damages for the pain and suffering of being alive at all was against public policy. [1982] Q.B. 1166

COMMENTARY

It was stated *obiter* that "wrongful life" claims could not be brought under the Congenital Disabilities (Civil Liability) Act 1976 because of the wording of section 1 (2) (b) which requires that when the negligence arises after conception that "the child is born with disabilities which would not otherwise have been present". It should be noted that in this case the claim was not for the disabilities but only for failing to give the mother the chance to have an abortion. The plaintiff's disabilities were caused by the rubella—not by the negligence of the hospital.

Key Principle: **Claims by parents for "wrongful birth" after the failure of negligently conducted sterilisations or abortions are recognised by the courts.**

Thake v. Maurice 1986

Mr Thake had a vasectomy operation which was carefully and competently performed by the defendant. The minute risk of natural reversal of the surgery materialised and three years later his wife conceived again. Believing her husband to be sterile she thought that she could not be pregnant and by the time the wife went to the doctor she was told that she was five months pregnant and too late for an abortion. The plaintiffs sued on the basis that the defendant had failed to warn them of the small chance that the vasectomy might reverse itself naturally.

HELD: (CA) The defendant was liable and the Court rejected the contention that public policy would bar the award of damages to parents following the birth of a healthy child after the father had undergone a vasectomy which was alleged to have been negligently performed. [1986] Q.B. 644

COMMENTARY

(1) In *Goodwill v. British Pregnancy Advisory Service*, *The Times*, January 29, 1996, the Court of Appeal held that no

duty of care was owed by the defendant, BPAS, to a man's future sexual partner who became pregnant and gave birth to a duaghter following the spontaneous reversal of his vasectomy.

(2) Initially, in *Udale v. Bloomsbury Area Health Authority* [1983] 2 All E.R. 522, where the defendant health authority accepted responsibility for a surgeon's negligent performance of a sterilisation operation, Jupp J. refused the mother compensation towards the upkeep of the child. He said the birth of a child was a blessing and the financial cost of such a blessing was irrecoverable. It offended society's notions of what was is right and the value afforded to human life, and the knowledge that his parents had claimed damages in respect of his birth might distress and damage the child emotionally as he grows to maturity.

(3) Jupp J. was overruled on the policy issue by the Court of Appeal in *Emeh v. Kensington Area Health Authority* [1985] Q.B. 1012, where their Lordships expressed a disinclination to place limits on the scope of the duty owed to the mother by reference to what was "socially unacceptable".

---

4. NEGLIGENCE: BREACH OF DUTY

The standard of care required by the common law is that of the reasonable man. This was defined in *Blyth v. Birmingham Waterworks Co.* (1856) 11 Ex. 781 as the omission to do something that a reasonable man would do or doing something which a reasonable and prudent man would not do. In *Glasgow Corporation v. Muir* [1943] A.C. 448 Lord Macmillan stated that this objective standard does not take account of the idiosyncrasies or weaknesses of the particular person whose conduct is in question. The question for the court is not did the defendant act reasonably, but in all the circumstances, would a reasonable person behave as the defendant did. It must then be proved by the plaintiff that, on the facts, the defendant's conduct fell below the appropriate standard. It is for the judge to decide what is reasonable or what could have been foreseen and the following cases will illustrate a number of guiding principles which are considered by the court.

Key Principle: **Where some precautions are required the standard of care that can reasonably be expected will vary according to the magnitude of the risk, the purpose of the defendant's activity and the practicability of precautions.**

Bolton v. Stone 1951
The plaintiff was standing in a quiet road when she was struck by a cricket ball which had been driven from the defendants' cricket ground. It was rare for balls to be hit out of the ground: only on about six occasions in 28 years had balls been hit out and no injury had resulted. Even though the risk of such an accident was foreseeable the chance that it would actually occur was very small. **HELD:** (HL) The defendants were not liable because in the circumstances it was reasonable to ignore such a small risk. [1951] A.C. 850

COMMENTARY
(1) In *Miller v. Jackson* [1977] Q.B. 966 by a majority the Court of Appeal held that the risk of harm was so great that the defendants were liable where cricket balls were hit out of their ground eight or nine times a season and, on numerous occasions, had damaged the plaintiff's property.
(2) In *Haley v. London Electricity Board* [1965] A.C. 778, HL, the defendant's servants who had been excavating a hole in the street took precautions for the protection of passersby. The precautions which were taken were adequate for sighted persons but not for the plaintiff who was blind and fell into the hole. The defendants were held liable because the presence of blind persons on the pavement was foreseeable and adequate precautions would have been simple to take.

Key Principle: **The obligations of a potential defendant may increase where the risk to a plaintiff is of greater damage than normal.**

Paris v. Stepney Borough Council 1951

The defendants knew that the plaintiff was blind in one eye. He was working in conditions which involved some risk of eye injury but the likelihood of this injury was not sufficient to call upon the defendants to provide goggles to a normal two-eyed workman. The plaintiff was rendered totally blind when a chip of metal entered his good eye.

HELD: (HL) The duty of employers was owed to each particular employee and they were negligent in failing to provide goggles to the plaintiff. In this case the risk to a two-eyed workman was the loss of one eye but the plaintiff risked the much greater injury of total blindness. [1951] A.C. 367

Key Principle: **The risk has to be balanced against the end to be achieved and, if sufficiently important, justifies the assumption of abnormal risk.**

Watt v. Hertfordshire County Council 1954

The plaintiff was a fireman called out to an emergency where a woman was trapped under a lorry. A heavy lifting jack was urgently required but, since a vehicle designed to carry this was not available, it was loaded onto a lorry which was not equipped to secure it. On the way to the scene of the accident the lorry had to brake suddenly and the plaintiff was injured when the jack slipped.

HELD: (CA) The fire authorities had not been negligent. The risk had to be balanced against the end to be achieved and the saving of life or limb justifies taking considerable risk. [1954] 1 W.L.R. 835; 2 All E.R. 368

COMMENTARY

Lord Denning took the view that if the accident had happened in a commercial venture without any emergency the plaintiff would have succeeded, but "the commercial end to make profit is very different from the human end to save life or limb."

Key Principle: The risk has to be weighed against the measures necessary to eliminate it.

Smith v. Littlewoods Ltd 1987

The defendants were the owners of a cinema which was left unoccupied and unguarded during the time it was awaiting redevelopment. When youths entered the premises and deliberately started a fire which spread to, and seriously damaged the plaintiffs' buildings next door, it was alleged that the defendants should have prevented access to the cinema. The defendants were not aware of the presence of the vandals and had no reason to assume that they constituted a significant threat.

HELD: The defendants were not liable. Short of posting a 24-hour guard over the property they would not have been in a position to prevent the vandals getting in. To require such a measure would impose an intolerable burden. [1987] A.C. 241

COMMENTARY
See also *Latimer v. A.E.C. Ltd* (1953) (see p. 84)

Key Principle: Where a person undertakes a task which requires a particular skill s/he will be judged by the standards of a person who is reasonably competent in the exercise of that skill.

Wells v. Cooper 1958

The plaintiff, who went to deliver fish to the defendant's house, was invited to stay for a cup of tea. After drinking the tea he was leaving the house by the back door when the door-handle came away in his hand. He fell to the ground from the back steps. The handle had been fitted a few months earlier by the defendant who had some experience as an amateur carpenter and who frequently did such jobs around the house.

HELD: (CA) The defendant had exercised such care as was required of him and was not liable. A householder who does some small repair about his house is not expected to show the skill of a professional carpenter working for reward: he need only do his work with the skill of a reasonably competent carpenter doing the work in question. [1958] 2 Q.B. 265

COMMENTARY
The degree of skill was not to be measured by the skill which the defendant personally happened to possess, but by

reference to the degree of care and skill which a reasonably competent carpenter might apply to the work in question.

Key Principle: The test for competence is objective: there is no variable standard for different levels of experience, competence or temperament.

Nettleship v. Weston 1971

The plaintiff was teaching the defendant to drive. During the course of the defendant's third lesson, she panicked and steered the car into a lamppost and the plaintiff suffered a broken knee cap. At first instance the trial judge decided that the plaintiff had not been at fault because she had been doing her best to control the car. **HELD:** (CA) The Court of Appeal disagreed with the trial judge and held that the standard of care required of a learner-driver is the same as that of the ordinary qualified driver. The defendant's driving had fallen below this standard and it was irrelevant that this was because of her inexperience. According to Lord Denning: "A learner driver may be doing his best but his incompetent best is not good enough". [1971] 2 Q.B. 691

COMMENTARY

(1) In *Roberts v. Ramsbottom* [1980] 1 W.L.R. 823 the defendant, who suffered a stroke which severely impaired his consciousness, continued to drive for some distance and collided with two vehicles in succession. He was found liable because he had retained some control and a prudent person would have stopped driving under such circumstances. His illness would only have provided a defence if it had rendered his actions wholly beyond his control so as to amount to automatism.

(2) In *Wilsher v. Essex Area Health Authority* [1988] 1 All E.R. 871 the Court of Appeal rejected the argument that a junior inexperienced doctor owed a lower duty of care. Glidwell L.J. commented: "the law requires the trainee or learner to be judged by the same standard as his more experienced colleagues. If it did not, inexperience would frequently be urged as a defence to an action for professional negligence." (This point was not raised on appeal to the House of Lords [1988] 2 W.L.R. 557) (see p. 49)

Key Principle: The appropriate test for judging the standard of professional behaviour is not that of the ordinary man: the defendant is judged by the standard of the ordinary skilled person exercising and professing to have that special skill.

Bolam v. Friern Hospital Management Committee 1957
The plaintiff agreed to undergo electro-convulsive therapy (ECT) during which he suffered a fracture to the pelvis. The issue was whether the doctor was negligent in failing to give a relaxant drug before the treatment, or in failing to provide means of restraint during the procedure. Evidence was given of the practices of various doctors in the use of relaxant drugs before ECT treatment. One body of medical opinion favoured the use of relaxant drugs, but another body of opinion took the view that they should not be used because of the risk of fractures.
HELD: The action failed. A defendant is not negligent if he acts in accordance with a practice accepted at the time as proper by a responsible body of professional opinion skilled in the particular form of treatment. [1957] 2 All E.R. 118

COMMENTARY
(1) In *Bolito v. City and Hacknet HA* (see p. 48) although the issue was one of causation, the medical experts had disagreed as to whether a doctor ought to have intubated the plaintiff. The court said that whether it would have been a breach of duty not to intubate had to be decided by applying the *Bolam* test. However, the House of Lords emphasised that ultimately it was for the court, and not for medical opinion, to decide what was the standard of care required in each case. The court had to be satisfied that the opinion had a logical basis, which would involve the weighing of risks against benefits, in order to reach a defensible conclusion.
(2) This test, set down in a High Court decision and approved by the House of Lords (see below), is of general application and not limited to doctors. In *Luxmoore-May v. Messenger May Baverstock* [1990] 1 All E.R. 1067, the test was applied to a firm of provincial auctioneers valuing a painting for a client prior to sale. The defendant auctioneers were "general practitioners" and were not liable for failing to identify a valuable painting in circumstances where a specialist London firm would have been held negligent.
(3) The test is not conclusive. A common professional practice will sometimes be condemned as unreasonable. The courts take the view that neglect of duty does not cease by

repetition to be neglect of duty: in *Re The Herald of Free Enterprise*, *The Independent*, December 18, 1987, there was ample evidence that most ferries set sail with their bow doors open. The Divisional Court held that this was not evidence of the required standard of care but rather of a general and culpable complacency in respect of elementary safety precautions.

Key Principle: The *Bolam* test applies to treatment and clinical judgement.

Whitehouse v. Jordan 1981

The defendant, a senior registrar, had delivered the plaintiff baby. The birth was a difficult one and it was alleged that the defendant had pulled too long and too hard in attempting a forceps delivery before eventually performing a Caesarean section. This had resulted in severe brain damage to the plaintiff for which the trial judge held the doctor liable.

HELD: (HL) The defendant was not negligent as the evidence did not establish that the doctor had departed from accepted practice. [1981] 1 All E.R. 267

COMMENTARY

The House of Lords emphatically re-stated the *Bolam* test and rejected the argument that there was a difference between an error of judgment and negligence. In the Court of Appeal Lord Denning had argued: "When I give a judgment and it is afterwards reversed by the House of Lords, is it to be said that I was negligent?" According to Lord Edmund-Davies:

> "To say that a surgeon committed an error of clinical judgment is wholly ambiguous, for while some such errors may be completely consistent with the due exercise of professional skill, other acts or omissions in the course of exercising 'clinical judgment' may be so glaringly below proper standards as to make a finding of negligence inevitable."

Key Principle: The *Bolam* test applies to making a diagnosis and where there is conflicting medical opinion a doctor is not negligent merely because there is a body of opinion that takes a contrary view.

Maynard v. West Midlands Regional Health Authority 1984

A consultant physician and a surgeon were uncertain whether the plaintiff was suffering from tuberculosis or from Hodgkin's disease. Hodgkin's disease can be fatal unless treated early so they carried out an operation before obtaining test results which would have determined her illness. The operation carries an inherent risk of damage to the vocal cords and this risk materialised in the plaintiff. She claimed that the consultants were negligent in carrying out the operation before the test results were available.

HELD: (HL) The defendants were held not to be negligent. Although there was a body of competent opinion which said that the consultants' decision was wrong there was an equally competent body which supported their approach. [1984] 1 W.L.R. 634

COMMENTARY

Lord Scarman stated the justification for the *Bolam* test in the following terms:

> ". . . a judge's 'preference' for one body of distinguished professional opinion over another, also professionally distinguished is not sufficient to establish negligence."

Key Principle: A defendant is not expected to have anticipated future developments in knowledge or practice but will be judged by reference to the state of knowledge at the time of the event.

Roe v. Ministry of Health 1954

The two plaintiffs entered hospital for minor surgery and emerged permanently paralysed from the waist down. Anaesthetic which was injected spinally during the course of the operation had become contaminated by seepage through invisible cracks in the glass. At the time of the accident in 1947 the risk of this seepage occurring was not known.

HELD: (CA) It was not negligent for the defendant not to have known of the danger. Lord Denning warned that it so easy to be wise after the event and said, "We must not look at the 1947 accident with 1954 spectacles." [1954] 2 Q.B. 66

Key Principle: The *Bolam* test applies to the disclosure of information by doctors to patients about risks of proposed procedures.

Sidaway v. Bethlem Royal Hospital Governors 1985

The plaintiff agreed to undergo an operation to her spine in order to relieve pain in her right arm and shoulder. She was not informed that the operation carried a risk (of less than 1 per cent) that she would suffer damage to the spine. The operation was performed without negligence but unfortunately the risk materialised and the plaintiff became severely disabled. She sued the defendants on the ground that the surgeon had failed to inform her of the risk.

HELD: (HL) The defendants were not liable. The surgeon had followed approved practice of neurosurgeons in not disclosing the risk of damage to the spinal cord and was not negligent. [1985] 1 All E.R. 643

COMMENTARY

The contention that the standard of care ought to be what the reasonable patient would want to know, rather than what the reasonable doctor was prepared to tell, was rejected by the court. In failing to adopt the doctrine of "informed consent" which operates in other jurisdictions and allows the patient access to full and frank information about treatment and prognoses the English courts leave discretion to the professional judgment of the doctor regarding the disclosure of information.

Key Principle: Children are to be judged against the standard of the ordinary child of the same age.

McHale v. Watson 1966

The defendant, a boy of twelve, threw a pointed steel rod at a wooden post. It glanced off the post and struck the plaintiff in the eye.

HELD: The defendant was not liable in negligence. The standard of care is adjusted for the child's age and is therefore such a standard as can reasonably be expected of an ordinary child of the same age as the defendant. (This is an Australian case—there is little authority in English law which deals with the position.) [1966] A.L.R. 513

COMMENTARY
Parents are generally not liable for the torts of their children. However, in circumstances where failure of the parent to supervise a child adequately results in injury to the child or a third party, the parent may be personally liable in negligence. Similarly, teachers may be responsible for failure to supervise children, in *Carmarthenshire County Council v. Lewis* [1955] A.C. 549 the House of Lords held a school authority liable where a four-year old child, left unattended in a classroom, wandered on to a road. A lorry driver was killed trying to avoid him, and it was held that under the circumstances it was reasonably foreseeable that the child would cause an accident.

Res ipsa loquitur

There has been disagreement in the courts about the exact effect of the maxim *res ipsa loquitur* and it had been argued that it shifted the burden of proof to the defendant. However, in *Ng Chun Pui v. Lee Chuen Tat* (1988) R.T.R. 298, the Privy Council stated that the burden of proof does not shift to the defendant and that the doctrine ". . . is no more than the use of a Latin maxim to describe the state of the evidence from which it is proper to draw an inference of negligence."

Key Principle: The facts of the accident itself may give rise to a *res ipsa loquitur* inference if the following three conditions are met:

(i) the defendant must have had sole control of the thing that caused the damage;

(ii) the accident could not have occurred without lack of proper care;

(iii) there is no other direct evidence of what caused the accident.

Scott v. London and St. Katherine Docks Co. 1865
The plaintiff, who was standing near the doorway of the defendants warehouse, was struck when several bags of sugar fell from a hoist. The defendant's employees had been using a hoist nearby to load sugar.
HELD: The plaintiff succeeded. In establishing liability on the part of the defendants there must be reasonable evidence of negligence, but if the three conditions above apply ". . . it affords reasonable evidence, in the absence of explanation by the defendant, that the accident arose from want of care." (1865) 3 H. & C. 596

COMMENTARY
The Civil Evidence Act 1968 provides that, unless the contrary is proved, the burden of proof in negligence shall be reversed where a person is proved to have been convicted of an offence.

Key Principle: To establish if the defendant has control of the situation which caused the damage, the test is whether outside interference was likely.

Easson v. London and North Eastern Railway Company 1944
The plaintiff, a four-year-old boy, fell through a door of a corridor train during the journey from Edinburgh to London.
HELD: The defendant did not have sufficient control over the door for the doctrine of *res ipsa loquitur* to apply. It was impossible to say that the doors of an express train were continuously under the control of the railway company: passengers could have interfered with the doors. [1944] K.B. 421

COMMENTARY
If it is improbable that some unauthorised person could have interfered with the thing that caused the damage the defendant has sufficient control. In *Gee v. Metropolitan Railway* (1873) L.R. 8 Q.B. 161, the plaintiff fell from a local train when the door flew open a few minutes after it had left the station. This was held to be evidence of negligence on the part of the railway company.

Key Principle: For *res ipsa loquitur* to apply it must be shown that the accident could not have occurred without negligence.

Cassidy v. Ministry of Health 1951
The plaintiff went into hospital to have treatment for two stiff fingers. On leaving hospital he had four stiff fingers and a useless hand.
HELD: (CA) This should not have happened if due care had been used and the doctrine applied. [1951] 2 K.B. 343

Key Principle: For *res ipsa loquitur* to apply there must be no evidence of the actual cause of the accident.

Barkway v. South Wales Transport Co. Ltd 1950
The plaintiff was travelling as a passenger in the defendants' bus. He was killed when a tyre burst and the bus veered across the road and went over an embankment. It was established that the cause of the accident was a defect in one of the tyres which might have been discovered beforehand.
HELD: (HL) As the cause of the accident was known *res ipsa loquitur* did not apply. (However, the defendant's negligence was established on the facts of the case.) [1950] 1 All E.R. 392

---

5. NEGLIGENCE: DAMAGE

Causation and Remoteness

The principles of causation and remoteness of damage are common to all torts. However, they are dealt with in this chapter because most of the cases on the subject have involved the tort of negligence. In order to prove damage the plaintiff must first show that the harm suffered was as a matter of fact caused by the defendant's breach of duty. This element is known as *causation in fact* and if "but for" the defendant's negligent conduct the damage would not have happened then that negligence is the cause of the damage. Where causation in fact is established the question of remoteness of damage then arises. This is known as *causation in law* and liability may still be avoided if the defendant can show that the damage suffered was too remote a consequence of the breach of duty.

Key Principle: **If the harm to the plaintiff would not have occurred "but for" the defendant's breach of duty then that negligence is a cause of the harm.**

Barnett v. Chelsea and Kensington Hospital Management Committee 1969

The plaintiff's husband was one of three night watchman who went to the defendant's hospital complaining of vomiting after drinking some tea. The nurse on duty consulted the casualty doctor by telephone and was instructed by him to tell the three men to go home to bed and to call their own doctors. Soon afterwards the plaintiff's husband died of arsenical poisoning. It was discovered that arsenic had been put into the tea of the workmen by persons unknown. There was no dispute that in failing to examine the plaintiff the doctor was negligent: the issue to be decided was whether the doctor's breach of duty had caused the man's death.

HELD: The claim failed. The hospital was able produce evidence to show that even if the deceased had been examined and treated with proper care he would still have died. Since the death would have occurred in any event the defendant's breach of duty was not a factual cause. [1969] 1 Q.B. 428

COMMENTARY

(1) This case established what is known as the "but for" test. Even though the test is widely applied it is not always adequate as, for example, where there are multiple causes of the plaintiff's damage.

(2) The "but for" test was applied in *Robinson v. Post Office* [1974] 2 All E.R. 737. The plaintiff sought medical treatment following a leg injury sustained through the defendant's negligence. During the treatment he suffered a serious reaction to an anti-tetanus vaccination which was administered by a doctor who omitted to test for the allergy. The defendant was held liable for this injury also: the doctor was not liable for his omission to test for an allergic reaction

because the vaccination was urgently needed and the test would not have revealed the allergy in time.

Key Principle: In a case of breach of duty by omission, such as the failure of a doctor to attend a patient, it is necessary to decide what would have happened had the defendant's duty been discharged. Whether the doctor's failure to attend causes the plaintiff's damage depends on what the doctor would have done had s/he turned up.

Bolito v. City and Hackney Health Authority 1997

The plaintiff, a two-year-old patient in the defendant's hospital, suffered respiratory failure and cardiac arrest from which he subsequently died. It was accepted that, having been called on more than one occasion by a nursing sister, one of the doctors was in breach of her duty to attend the child. The issue before the court was causation: did this breach of duty cause the plaintiff's injuries? Whether the doctor's failure to attend caused the plaintiff's damage depended on what she would have done had she turned up. If the plaintiff had been intubated (to provide an airway) the respiratory difficulties would not have resulted in cardiac arrest. However, the doctor who failed to respond said that even if she had attended she would not have intubated, and therefore the cardiac arrest would have occurred in any event (no "but for" causation). Both the plaintiff and the defendant called distinguished medical experts in determining whether the professional standard of care required any doctor who attended the plaintiff to intubate.

HELD: The action failed on the ground of causation. The House of Lords accepted that if the doctor had attended, her failure to intubate would not have been negligent because it was supported by a responsible body of professional opinion.

Key Principle: **If the plaintiff cannot positively prove that the defendant's breach of duty caused the damage it is sufficient to show that the defendant's negligent conduct made the injury more probable.**

McGhee v. National Coal Board 1973

The plaintiff worked at the defendant's brick kilns where the conditions were hot and dusty. The brick dust adhered to his sweaty skin and because his employer failed to provide washing facilities the plaintiff had to cycle home with his body still caked in brick dust. He contracted dermatitis and alleged that if washing facilities had been provided he would not have developed the disease. The medical evidence was unable to show that had washing facilities been provided the plaintiff would have escaped the disease. However, the evidence did show that the provision of showers would have materially reduced the risk of dermatitis.

HELD: (HL) The defendants were liable on the ground that it was sufficient for a plaintiff to show that the defendants' breach of duty made the risk of injury more probable even though it was uncertain whether it was the actual cause. [1973] 1 W.L.R. 1

COMMENTARY

This case was distinguished in *Wilsher v. Essex Area Health Authority* [1988] 1 All E.R. 871, where a premature baby was negligently given excessive oxygen. It is known that excessive oxygen given to premature babies can lead to blindness and the plaintiff alleged that this was the cause of his blindness. But there were up to five possible causes of the plaintiff's injury, any one of which might have caused his blindness. The House of Lords held that the burden of proof remained with the plaintiff who must establish that the defendant's breach of duty was at least a material contributory cause of the harm. Showing the defendant's negligence to be one out of five possible causes of the plaintiff's blindness was not evidence that it was the cause. In *McGhee* the plaintiff had established his disease was caused by the brick dust: the only question was whether the additional period of exposure to the brick dust had contributed to the his dermatitis.

Key Principle: The plaintiff must prove, on the balance of probabilities, that damage was caused by the defendant's breach of duty.

Hotson v. East Berkshire Area Health Authority 1987

The plaintiff was rushed to hospital when he suffered a hip injury following a fall from a tree. The damage to his hip created a 75 per cent chance that he would develop a permanent disability. The defendants negligently failed to correctly diagnose the plaintiff's hip condition and it went untreated for five days. By the time the mistake was discovered permanent disability was inevitable. The trial judge found that the delayed treatment had deprived the plaintiff of a 25 per cent chance of recovery and he awarded 25 per cent of the full compensation.

HELD: (HL) In reversing the decision it was held that there was no basis in tort for the judge's decision to award damages for loss of "chance" of complete recovery. If the plaintiff could prove, on the balance of probabilities, that he would have recovered if given proper treatment he was entitled to full compensation. Otherwise he was entitled to nothing. [1987] A.C. 750

COMMENTARY

The decision of the judge at first instance was upheld by the Court of Appeal [1987] A.C. 750. The question of whether it would ever be possible to recover in tort for a lost chance was left open by the House of Lords. However, in *Allied Maples Group Ltd v. Simmons & Simmons* [1995] 1 W.L.R. 1602 the Court of Appeal confirmed a first instance decision that a plaintiff can succeed if a real and substantial rather than speculative chance can be shown: the principle of the contract case *Chaplin v. Hicks* [1911] 2 K.B. 786 was applied.

Key Principle: Where two independent events cause the damage, and the second defendant's breach produces the same damage as that caused by the first defendant, the first event should be treated as the cause.

Baker v. Willoughby 1970

In a road accident caused by the defendant's negligence the plaintiff suffered an injury to his left leg. Before the trial of his negligence action the plaintiff was the victim of an armed robbery at his place of work. He suffered gunshot wounds to his left leg and as a result of his injuries his leg had to be amputated. The defendant admitted negligence but argued that his responsibility ended when the plaintiff was shot and therefore all losses from the date of the shooting flowed from the robbery.

HELD: The court rejected the defendant's argument on the ground that it produced a manifest injustice and held that he remained liable for the full extent of the plaintiff's damage. H.L. [1970] A.C. 467

COMMENTARY

Similar facts arose in *Jobling v. Associated Dairies Ltd* [1981] 2 All E.R. 752 where the defendants were liable in negligence when the plaintiff sustained a back injury at his place of work. This injury led to a 50 per cent reduction in his earning capacity. Three years later, and before his negligence action, the onset of a disease of the spine rendered the plaintiff totally unfit for work. But in this case the second event was brought about by natural causes and the House of Lords held that the defendants were only liable for the reduced earning capacity up to the time of the onset of the disease.

Intervening Cause

Novus Actus Interveniens

Key Principle: Where it can be established that an intervening act—a *novus actus interveniens*—has caused the damage, it may break the causal link between the defendant's breach of duty and the damage.

McKew v. Holland & Hannon & Cubbitts 1969

Through the defendant's negligence the plaintiff suffered an injury and for a short time afterwards he occasionally lost control of his leg. He went to inspect a flat and, without asking for assistance, he attempted to descend a steep flight of stairs with no handrail. When his leg gave way without warning he fell and sustained further injuries.

HELD: (HL) The defendant's were not liable for his additional injury because *the plaintiff's own act* broke the chain of causation. By placing himself in a position which might involve such a risk his own conduct had been unreasonable. [1969] 3 All E.R. 1621

COMMENTARY
(1) Similar facts arose in *Weiland v. Cyril Lord Carpets* [1969] 3 All E.R. 1006 where the plaintiff had been negligently injured and forced to wear a surgical collar. This restricted her ability to focus her bifocal glasses and as a result she sustained further injuries when she fell down some steps. But here the defendants were found liable because the plaintiff had not acted unreasonably in attempting to descend the steps.
(2) In *Pigney v. Pointers Transport* (see p. 000) a suicide which resulted from a negligently inflicted head injury was held not to break the chain of causation.

Key Principle: Where the subsequent event is the *intervening act of a third party*, negligent conduct is more likely to break the chain of causation than conduct which is not.

Knightley v. Johns 1982
The defendant's negligent driving caused the blocking of a busy road tunnel. A police inspector sent the plaintiff police constable to drive back against the traffic flow to close the tunnel entrance. As he was driving back into the tunnel the plaintiff was injured by a car being driven the other way.
HELD: (CA) The defendant was not liable. While it might be natural, probable and foreseeable that police would come to deal with the accident and that there might be risk taking, there were so many errors before the plaintiff was sent back into the tunnel that the police inspector's negligent behaviour was the cause of the plaintiff's injuries. [1982] 1 W.L.R. 349

COMMENTARY
When a tort occurs first *a subsequent act of nature* may supervene and break the chain of causation. In *Carslogie Steamship Co. Ltd v. Royal Norwegian Government* [1952] A.C. 292 the plaintiff's ship was damaged in a collision caused by the defendant's negligence. Having set out on a voyage she would not have made had the collision not occurred, she suffered extensive damage due to heavy weather conditions. The defendants were not liable for the weather damage which was held to be an intervening event in the ordinary course of the voyage. The tort was merely part

of the history of events which placed the ship in that place at that time.

Remoteness of Damage/Causation in Law

Key Principle: Where a duty of care is owed a defendant is liable for all the direct consequences of negligent conduct, no matter how unusual or unexpected.

Re Polemis and Furness, Withy & Co. 1921

Stevedores unloading a ship at Cassablanca negligently let a plank fall into the hold in which a cargo of cans containing petrol was stored. A spark ignited petrol vapour and caused an explosion in which the ship was destroyed.

HELD: (CA) The defendants were liable for the loss of the ship because it was a direct, although not a foreseeable consequences of their negligence. Scrutton L.J. observed that "once the act is negligent, the fact that its exact operation was not foreseen is immaterial." [1921] 3 K.B. 560

COMMENTARY

Re Polemis was strongly criticised by the Privy Council who refused to follow it in *The Wagon Mound* (see below). Foreseeability of damage has been adopted by subsequent courts as the test of remoteness of damage in negligence.

Key Principle: The defendant is not liable for all the direct losses: the *kind* of harm sustained by the plaintiff must be reasonably foreseeable.

Overseas Tankship (U.K.) Ltd v. Morts Dock and Engineering Co. Ltd, The Wagon Mound, 1961

Owing to the carelessness of the defendants a large quantity of fuel oil was discharged from their ship into Sydney Harbour. The oil was carried by wind and tide to the plaintiff's wharf about 600 feet away where welding on another ship was being carried out. After making enquiries the plaintiffs were advised that it was safe to continue with the welding operations on their wharf. Two days later the oil caught fire and the wharf and the ships being repaired were damaged in the blaze. The oil also congealed on the slipways and interfered with the plaintiff's use of the slips. Because there was a breach of duty and direct damage, at trial and at appeal, following *Re Polemis*, judgment was given for the plaintiff.

HELD: The Privy Council reversed the decision. The fact that some of the damage suffered (the damage to the slipways) was foreseeable did not make the defendants liable for the fire damage which was unforeseeable. The test for remoteness of damage was whether the *kind* of damage sustained was reasonably foreseeable. The Court also stated that *Re Polemis* should no longer be regarded as good law. [1961] A.C. 388

Key Principle: If the kind of damage suffered is reasonably foreseeable, the precise manner in which it occurred need not have been.

Hughes v. Lord Advocate 1963

Employees of the Post Office negligently left an open manhole unattended in the street. It was covered by a canvas tent and surrounded by paraffin warning lamps. Out of curiosity two young boys entered the tent and the plaintiff, a boy aged eight, took one of the lamps in with him. The lamp was knocked into the hole and caused a violent explosion in which the plaintiff suffered severe burns.

HELD: (HL) The defendants were held liable. Even though in the circumstances the explosion was unforeseeable the kind of damage which occurred, burns, was of a type which was foreseeable. [1963] A.C. 837

COMMENTARY

This case was distinguished by the Court of Appeal in *Doughty v. Turner Manufacturing Company Ltd* [1964] 1 Q.B. 518 where an asbestos cover was knocked into a cauldron of molten liquid. A minute or two later, due to a chemical reaction which was unforeseeable at the time, the liquid erupted and the plaintiff suffered burns. The plaintiff failed on the ground that a splash causing burns was foreseeable the but the damage which occurred was of an entirely different kind.

Key Principle: Provided that the type of harm and its occurrence are reasonably foreseeable it is irrelevant that the damage is more extensive than could have been foreseen.

Vacwell Engineering Co. Ltd v. B.D.H. Chemicals Ltd 1971

The defendants negligently failed to warn the plaintiffs that a chemical which they supplied was liable to cause an explosion if mixed with water. The plaintiff's employee allowed the chemical to come into contact with water and the reaction led to an explosion of unforeseeable violence which destroyed much of the plaintiff's premises.

HELD: (CA) The defendants were liable: it was no defence that an explosion much greater in magnitude than was foreseeable had resulted. [1971] 1 Q.B. 111

Key Principle: The amount of damage that a victim suffers as the result of negligence depends upon the individual's characteristics and constitution. This is known as the "egg–shell skull" principle: tort-feasors must take their victims as they find them.

Smith v. Leech Brain & Co. 1962

The plaintiff employee suffered a burn to his lip as a result of inadequate safety measures in the defendant employer's factory. The plaintiff's lip was in a pre-malignant condition and the burn caused him to develop cancer which ultimately led to his death. The defendants argued that it was not reasonably foreseeable that the plaintiff would suffer cancer from being burned.

HELD: The defendants were liable, even though the only foreseeable injury was a splash causing a burn the "egg-shell skull" rule applied. The question to be asked was whether the burn could be foreseen: not whether the cancer was foreseeable. [1962] 2 Q.B. 405

COMMENTARY

(1) In *Robinson v. Post Office* the plaintiff's damage was a combination of the defendant's negligence and the administration of medical treatment to which he was allergic. Applying the "egg-shell skull" rule the defendant was held liable for both the original injury and the allergic reaction to the injection.

(2) The rule was also applied in *Pigney v. Pointers Transport Services Ltd* [1957] 2 All E.R. 807. The defendant's

negligence caused a severe head injury which induced a depressive mental illness in the plaintiff's husband. It was the victim's reaction to this illness which led to his suicide and the defendants were held liable.

Key Principle: The "egg-shell skull principle" applies to cases of "nervous shock" as it does to any other type of injury.

Brice v. Brown 1984

A plaintiff and her nine-year old daughter were passengers in a taxi which was involved in a collision with a bus. The daughter suffered minor injuries. Even though the physical injuries sustained by the mother were trivial, owing to a pre-existing personality disorder, she suffered a hysterical reaction and lasting nervous shock resulting from the injuries suffered by her daughter. **HELD:** The test is whether it is foreseeable that a person of normal disposition and phlegm might suffer nervous shock through the risk created by the defendant's negligence. The plaintiff was allowed to succeed on the basis that a person of customary phlegm would have suffered nervous shock in these circumstances and the defendant's argument—that the plaintiff's unusual and exceptional reaction to the accident was unforeseeable—was rejected. [1984] 1 All E.R. 997

COMMENTARY

In *Page v. Smith* [1995] 2 W.L.R. 644, the House of Lords held that in claims for nervous shock it is necessary to distinguish between primary and secondary victims. Where the plaintiff is a primary victim, personal injury of some kind must be foreseeable, but it is not necessary to show that injury by shock was foreseeable. Where the plaintiff is a secondary victim the defendant will not be liable unless psychiatric injury is foreseeable in a person of normal fortitude.

---

6. SPECIAL DUTY SITUATIONS

Nervous Shock

Introduction

Claims for nervous shock, which are not the result of physical injury to the plaintiff, are dealt with separately from claims for ordinary physical damage. Physical damage caused by negligence will be limited to those within the range of the harmful event, but nervous shock may affect a wide range of persons beyond the direct victim of negligent conduct. Therefore, the courts have adopted a cautious and restrictive approach to the imposition of liability. For example, in *Victorian Railway Commissioners v. Coultas* (1888) 12 App. Cas. 222 it was held that such damage was not compensable at all. Initially there was judicial scepticism about the existence of nervous shock as a medical condition and a fear of fraudulent claims. There was also the fear that if such actions were allowed to succeed the "floodgates" would open to allow a rush of claims. Changing judicial attitudes to claims for nervous shock—or psychiatric injury, which is the term now preferred—are reflected in the following cases. In such claims the courts have been reluctant to apply the foreseeability principle of negligence and have imposed a number of specific restrictions on the law beyond reasonable foreseeability.

Key Principle: **Where psychiatric injury is sustained through fear for the plaintiff's *own safety* there is no need for physical impact to establish a claim for nervous shock.**

Dulieu v. White 1901
The plaintiff, a pregnant woman, was working behind the bar of a public house when the defendant ran his van and horses through the window. She was not physically injured but was badly frightened and this resulted in the premature birth of her child.
HELD: The plaintiff was entitled to recover because there was real and immediate fear of injury to herself. [1901] 2 K.B. 669

COMMENTARY
(1) The recovery of damages was limited to "shock which arises from a reasonable fear of immediate personal injury to oneself."
(2) A bystander who witnesses a particularly horrific event without fear of personal harm is not owed a duty of care. In *McFarlane v. E.E. Caledonia Ltd* [1994] 2 All E.R. 1, the plaintiff suffered shock as a result of witnessing the fire on Piper Alpha drilling platform in which 164 men were killed. His claim failed on the grounds that: he was a mere by-stander and was not in fear for his own safety; he had no close relationship of love and affection with those in danger; nor was he actively involved in the rescue operations.

Key Principle: Shock which results from what is seen or per-ceived by a plaintiff's own *unaided senses* is recoverable: there is no action in respect of shock sustained as a result of what a plaintiff has been told by others.

Hambrook v. Stokes Bros 1925
The plaintiff witnessed the defendant's lorry going out of control and round a bend just where she had left her children who were walking to school. Even though she did not see the collision which ensued, she feared for the safety of her children. She was subse-quently told that a child fitting the description of her daughter might have been injured in the accident. The plaintiff eventually died from the shock.
HELD: (CA)

   (1) The shock suffered by the plaintiff was induced by what she had seen by her own eyes rather than what she had been told and the defendants were liable. The limitation in *Dulieu v. White*—that in order to succeed a plaintiff had to fear for his or her own safety—was rejected on the ground that to allow this would deny a remedy to a mother who feared for the safety of her children in circumstances where a plaintiff who thought only of her own safety could recover. [1925] 1 K.B. 141
   (2) The effect of this decision was to limit claims to plaintiffs who were in close physical proximity to the accident although it was not essential that they had seen the accident itself. The "sight and sound" requirement was extended in

McLoughlin v. O'Brian (see below) include the "aftermath"
of the accident.

Key Principle: When applying the test of foreseeability of injury
by shock, it has to be shown that the plaintiff is a person of
reasonable fortitude and not particularly vulnerable to some
form of psychiatric reaction.

Bourhill v. Young 1943

The plaintiff, an Edinburgh fishwife, had just alighted from a tram
when she heard the impact of an accident involving a tram and a
motorcyclist. This occurred some fifty feet away on the other side
of the tram and outside her line of vision. She approached the site
of the accident and alleged that she suffered nervous shock and
gave birth to a stillborn child about a month later.

HELD: The House of Lords held that the plaintiff was owed no
duty of care. She was so far from the accident that she was in no
physical danger—whe was not within in the area of *impact*. The
nature of the relationship between the primary accident victim and
the plaintiff suffering the shock was relevant and Mrs Bourhill was
a *total stranger* to the primary victim. Furthermore, the ordinary
bystander can be expected to withstand the sight and sound of
road accidents. As a pregnant woman the plaintiff was considered
to be particularly vulnerable to mental trauma and therefore not
of *reasonable fortitude*. [1943] A.C. 92

COMMENTARY

Once *some* psychiatric harm is foreseeable to a person of
reasonable fortitude, then the particularly vulnerable plaintiff can recover. (See *Brice v. Brown*, p. 56.)

Key Principle: In claims for nervous shock it is necessary to
distinguish between primary and secondary victims. A "primary
victim" is a person directly involved as a participant in the accident and if personal injury of some kind is foreseeable, it is not
necessary to show that injury by shock was foreseeable. However,
where the plaintiff is a "secondary victim" (such as a witness to
the accident) the defendant will not be liable unless psychiatric
injury is foreseeable in a person of reasonable fortitude.

Page v. Smith 1996
The plaintiff was driving with due care when a car driven by the defendant turned into his path. This caused an accident of moderate severity and although there was damage to the cars, the plaintiff was physically unharmed in the collision. However, he had suffered from myalgic encephalomyelitis (ME) for 20 years which at the time of the accident was in remission. He claimed that the accident resulted in the reactivation of this condition.
HELD: Provided personal injury of some kind is foreseeable the defendant was liable for the psychiatric injury, irrespective of whether psychiatric injury was foreseeable. [1996] 1 A.C. 155

COMMENTARY
In the case of secondary victims, plaintiffs will be required to satisfy the "proximity requirements" set out in *Alcock* (see below).

Key Principle: **Liability for nervous shock extends to rescuers and the relationship with any of the victims is not relevant to the claim.**

Chadwick v. British Railways Board 1967
There was no danger to the plaintiff himself nor was he related to any of the victims of the train disaster for which the defendants were liable. In rescuing victims from the scene of the accident he witnessed horrific sights from which he suffered long-term psychiatric illness.
HELD: A duty was owed to rescuers. Injury and danger to the passengers could have been forseen as could injury to someone who was trying to rescue them. [1967] 1 W.L.R. 912

COMMENTARY
Permitting rescuers to recover for shock reflects judicial policy of accommodating such claims on the grounds that nothing should deter rescuers from acting in an emergency. However, no duty is owed to mere bystanders who are not actively taking part in the rescue operations. See *McFarlane v. E.E. Caledonia* (p. 58).

Key Principle: **In addition to reasonable foreseeability the plaintiff must be: a close relative of the victim; witness the accident or the immediate aftermath with unaided senses; be proximate in both time and space.**

McLoughlin v. O'Brian 1983

The defendant admitted liability for an accident in which the plaintiff's young daughter was killed and her husband and two other children suffered injuries. At the time of the accident the plaintiff was at home two miles away. She was informed of the accident an hour later and was driven to the hospital where her family had been taken. Upon arrival she was told of the death and saw the injuries to her family in distressing circumstances before they had been treated by medical staff. The plaintiff claimed for the nervous shock which she suffered as the result of these events.
HELD: (HL) The nervous shock had been the reasonably foreseeable result of injuries to her family and the defendants were liable. [1983] 1 A.C. 410

COMMENTARY

(1) This decision represented an extension of the existing law as the plaintiff was not at the scene of the accident.
(2) This case left the law in an uncertain state and it was arguable that the test for liability in nervous shock depended on foreseeability alone. Although the court unanimously agreed that the plaintiff's shock was readily foreseeable, the reasoning of their Lordships varied. Lord Bridge and Lord Scarman adopted a test based on foreseeeability alone and considered the question of whether, as a matter of policy there should be some other limit on the duty of care, to be inappropriate for the court. But Lord Wilberforce, with whom Lord Edmund-Davies agreed, were of the opinion that it was open to the court to decide the issue on grounds of policy. They adopted an "aftermath test"—foreseeability of shock was not sufficient, additional limits were required: close relationship with the victim; proximity in terms of time and space; shock from being told by a third party would not be compensated.

Key Principle: In addition to reasonable foreseeability of nervous shock the following factors must be considered: the relationship between the primary victim and the plaintiff; the proximity of the plaintiff in time and space to the scene of the accident; the means by which the shock has been caused.

Alcock v. Chief Constable of South Yorkshire 1992

Actions for nervous shock were brought against the police arising from the Hillsborough football stadium disaster. As the result of overcrowding, 95 people were crushed to death and hundreds more were injured. The tragedy was witnessed by thousands of fans at the match and others witnessed the horrific events on live television broadcasts. Claims were brought by relatives and friends of the victims who suffered psyciatric illness as a result of their experiences. A number of them had been in other parts of the stadium from where they had witnessed the events and others had seen the disaster live on television. Some of the plaintiffs had identified bodies at the mortuary and others suffered solely from being told the news. The plaintiffs based their claim on the argument that the sole test for a duty in nervous shock was reasonable foreseeability.

HELD: (HL) This argument was rejected and the plaintiffs' actions were dismissed. The House of Lords applied Lord Wilberforce's "aftermath test" in *McLoughlin v. O'Brian.* [1992] 1 A.C. 310

COMMENTARY

(1) The class of persons who would sue was not limited to spouse and parent-child relâtionships: the crucial factor was the existence of a sufficiently close tie of love and affection with the primary victim.

(2) Sight or sound of the accident will continue to satisfy the proximity test but their Lordships did not define immediate aftermath: in this case identifying a body in the mortuary eight hours after the incident was not within the immediate aftermath.

(3) The live television broadcast was found not to equate with the "sight or hearing of the event or its immediate aftermath" because the television authorities had followed the broadcasting code of ethics. Pictures of suffering by recognisable individuals had not been shown. However, the showing of such pictures could constitute a *novus actus interveniens* and break the chain of causation between the original breach of duty and the psychiatric illness.

Key Principle: (1) **An employee, who suffers psychiatric damage as a consequence of what is done to others, is not to be accorded special treatment in determining liability. In such cases the employee is a secondary victim and, as such, is subject to the "control mechanisms" in** *Alcock.*
(2) **In considering whether liability for psychiatric injury should be extended to rescuers it is legitimate to take into account that many will be from occupations in which they are trained and required to run such risks.**

White and Others v. Chief Constable of South Yorkshire Police and Others, 1998

Four police officers who were actively helping to deal with the human consequences of the Hillsborough tragedy claimed for the post traumatic stress disorder they suffered as the result of their experiences. They argued that there was no justification for regarding physical and psychiatric injury as different kinds of damage. It was also contended the employer was under the conventional employer's liability principles to protect employees from harm through work. In addition, three of the officers claimed as rescuers and argued that as such they were not subject to the control mechanisms in *Alcock.*
HELD:

(1) Nowadays courts accepted that there was no rigid distinction between body and mind and in that sense there was no qualitative difference between physical and psychiatric harm. However, it would be an altogether different proposition to say that no distinction was made or ought to be made between principles governing the recovery of damages in tort for physical injury and psychiatric harm. Policy considerations had undoubtedly played a part in shaping the law in this area. To allow the claims of the police officers would substantially expand the existing categories in which compensation could be recovered for pure psychiatric harm. Moreover, the awarding of damages to them sat uneasily with the denial of the claims to bereaved relatives by the decision in *Alcock.*

(2) The rules to be applied to an action against an employer for harm suffered in the workplace were governed by the ordinary rules of the law of tort and which contained restrictions on the recovery of compensation for psychiatric harm. The rules governing such recovery do not at present include police officers who sustained such injuries while on duty. If such a category were to be created by a judicial decision, the new principle would be available in many different

situations, for example, doctors and hospital workers who were exposed to grievous injuries and suffering. In addition, police officers who were traumatised by something in their work had the benefit of statutory schemes which permitted them to retire on pension. In that sense they were better off than the bereaved relatives in *Alcock*.

(3) None of the four police officers was at any time exposed to personal danger and none thought he was so exposed. In order to contain the concept of rescue in reasonable bounds the plaintiff must at least satisfy the threshold requirement that he objectively exposed himself to danger or reasonably believed that he was doing so. [1991] 1 All E.R. 1, HL

COMMENTARY
(1) The House of Lords allowed the appeal by the defendant against a Court of Appeal decision allowing the police officers to recover. The Court of Appeal had held that the plaintiffs, as rescuers, were to be singled out as a special category and it had also held that an employee was to be accorded special treatment in determining liability for nervous shock.
(2) The Law Commission made important proposals for reform in *Liability for Psychiatric Illness* (Law Com. No. 249, 1998)

Pure Economic Loss

Key Principle: Pure financial loss unaccompanied by any physical loss to person or property is not recoverable in tort.

Weller & Co. Ltd v. Foot and Mouth Disease Research Institute 1966
The plaintiffs, livestock auctioneers, were unable to continue their business because the defendants had negligently released a virus which caused an outbreak of foot and mouth disease in the area.
HELD: Farmers whose cattle contracted the disease were held to be owed a duty of care in negligence—their loss was recoverable. However, local auctioneers, who had suffered loss indirectly through loss of business were denied a remedy—their loss was purely economic. [1966] 1 Q.B. 569

COMMENTARY
The "floodgates" argument is prevalent in the restriction on recovery for pure economic loss and is justified by the undesirability to expose defendants to a potential liability "in an indeterminate amount for an indeterminate time to an

indeterminate class", *per* Cardozo C.J. in *Ultramares Corporation v. Touche* (1931) 174 N.E. 441.

Key Principle: There is a distinction between "pure economic loss" and economic loss which is consequent upon physical damage to person or property. Economic loss which results from physical damage is recoverable.

Spartan Steel & Alloys Ltd v. Martin & Co. (Contractors) Ltd 1973

The defendant contractor, in the course of digging the road, negligently cut a power cable causing the plaintiff's smelting works to be shut down. At the time of the power cut there was a "melt" in progress and to stop the steel solidifying it had to be drawn out of the furnace. This reduced its value by £368. The plaintiffs claimed for the reduced value of the melt and for the profit which would have been made had it been completed. They also claimed for the loss of profit from four further melts which would have been processed but for the fourteen hour power cut.

HELD: (CA) The plaintiffs recovered the reduction in the value of the solidified melt and the profits they would have made from its sale. However, they obtained nothing for the loss of profits on the four further melts which could have been processed before the electricity was restored: that was pure economic loss independent of the physical damage. [1973] Q.B. 27

COMMENTARY

Lord Denning made clear the public policy justifications for this decision. He stated: ". . . the risk of economic loss should be suffered by the whole community who suffer the losses—usually many but comparatively small losses—rather than on the one pair of shoulders . . ."

Key Principle: Where there is sufficient proximity between the parties there may be an exception to the rule that there is no recovery for loss which is not consequent upon physical loss.

Junior Books v. Veitchi Co. Ltd 1983

The plaintiff had employed the main contractors to construct a factory and they nominated the defendants, as specialist sub-

---

contractors, to lay the floor. The plaintiff alleged that the floor was defective (though not dangerous) and claimed the cost of replacing the floor plus consequential financial loss.

HELD: (HL) The defendants were liable, the proximity of the relationship between the parties was so close as to be as good as a contract and the building owner had, to the sub-contractor's knowledge, relied on his skill and experience. [1983]1 A.C. 520

COMMENTARY

It was also held that there was no question of indeterminate liability in this situation because the plaintiff was plainly foreseeable as an identified individual. However, this decision has not subsequently been followed and has been distinguished to the extent that it can be said to be unique to its own facts. In *Simaan General Contracting v. Pilkington Glass Ltd (No. 2)* [1988] Q.B. 758 Dillon L.J. stated, "I find it difficult to see that future citation from Junior Books can ever serve any useful purpose."

Key Principle: There is insufficient proximity between an ordinary purchaser and the manufacturer of defective products to impose a duty of care in respect of pure economic loss.

Muirhead v. Industrial Tank Specialities Ltd 1986

The plaintiff planned to buy lobsters when they were cheap, store them in tanks, and to supply them when they were scarce and in high demand. The pumps in the tanks failed to function properly and the plaintiff's lobsters died. In attempting to repair the pumps the plaintiff also suffered economic loss.

HELD: The manufacturer of the pumps was liable for the loss of the lobsters (property damage) but not for the money spent on the pumps or the cost of attempting to repair them (pure economic loss). Notwithstanding the imposition of liability in the absence of a contract in *Junior Books* the Court of Appeal held that liability for economic loss arising from defective products falls within the scope of contract law. [1986] Q.B. 507

COMMENTARY

The above cases have considered pure economic loss resulting from negligent acts but it is important to note that that pure economic loss resulting from negligent misstatements is recoverable under the principle in *Hedley Byrne v. Heller* (1964) (see below) and is the subject of the next section.

Negligent Misstatement

Where negligent words cause direct physical harm the plaintiff need only prove that such harm was foreseeable, as was the case with the workman in *Clayton v. Woodman & Son (Builders)* [1962] 2 Q.B. 533, who was injured when an architect negligently instructed a bricklayer to remove the keystone of an archway. More recently, this finding has been approved by Lord Oliver in *Caparo Industries plc v. Dickman* (1990). But where negligent words cause pure economic loss the courts take a much more restrictive approach. This restriction is justified by Lord Pearce in *Hedley Byrne* on the basis that "... words are more volatile than deeds, they travel fast and far afield, they are used without being expended."

Key Principle: Liability for pure economic loss, without injury to person or property can arise in the making of negligent misstatements. But foreseeablity of the loss is not enough to establish a duty of care—additional requirements must be met before liability is imposed.

Hedley Byrne v. Heller 1964

The appellants, advertising agents, became doubtful about the financial status of one of their clients, Easipower Ltd. They made enquiries of the defendant bankers with whom Easipower had an account. The respondents replied, first orally and then in writing, that Easipower was financially sound. The appellants relied on this advice and suffered financial loss when Easipower went into liquidation.

HELD: A duty of care would arise in relation to statements where there is a "special relationship" between the giver and the recipient of the advice. [1964] A.C. 465

COMMENTARY

(1) The nature of a "special relationship" was not fully defined by the court but the requirements for its existence appeared to be:

(i)   a reliance by the plaintiff on the defendant's special
        skill and judgment;

(ii)   knowledge, or reasonable expectation of knowledge
        on the part of the defendant, that the plaintiff was
        relying on the statement;

(iii)   it was reasonable in the circumstances for the plain-
        tiff to rely on the defendant.

(2) The concept of "a voluntary assumption of responsibility" has subsequently been used to establish proximity in
determining the existence of a duty of care. This arises from
an undertaking either express or implied that the defendant
will exercise care in giving information or advice. However
doubt has been expressed as to whether this criterion was
necessary or useful. In *Smith v. Bush* (see p. 70) Lord Griffiths suggested that it is not a helpful or realistic test for
liability, but in *Henderson v. Merrett Syndicates Ltd* 1994,
Lord Goff said that the criticism of the concept of a voluntary assumption of responsibility in *Smith v. Bush* is mis-
placed (below p. 70).
(3) The duty of care under *Hedley Byrne* has been restated
in more restricted terms by the House of Lords in *Caparo
Industries v. Dickman* (see p. 71).

Henderson v. Merrett Syndicates 1995
A number of claims arising out of the near-collapse of the Lloyds
of London Insurance market were taken by Lloyd's syndicates
(known as "names") alleging negligence on the part of the underwriting agents. The underwriting agents argued that the position
with the names should be governed by the terms of the contracts
between the parties and not by the law of tort which favoured
some of the names because of the more advantageous limitation
period in tort. [1995] 2 A.C. 145
HELD: The managing agents had assumed a direct responsibility to the names and a prima facie duty of care arose. Accordingly,
subagents acting on behalf of indirect Lloyd's names owed a duty
of care to the names because they had assumed such responsibility.
This was so notwithstanding that the parties were not in a contractual relationship.

COMMENTARY

In *Williams v. Natural Life Health Foods Ltd* [1998] 2 All E.R. 577 the plaintiffs entered a contract with a company to franchise a health food store. The plaintiff's business was not a success and they sought to prove that the defendant had personally assumed responsibility for the negligent advice provided by the company (which had subsequently been wound up). Although it was held in this case the defendants had not personally assumed responsibility to the plaintiff, Lord Steyn said that the extended *Hedley Byrne* principle established in *Henderson* does not merely apply to negligent statements, but also covers the negligent performance of services and can even found a tort duty concurrently with contract.

Key Principle: Liability under the *Hedley Byrne* principle should be restricted to defendants where the prominent purpose of the business was giving the advice in question, or who claimed that they had the requisite expertise.

Mutual Life and Citizens Assurance Co. Ltd v. Evatt 1971

The plaintiff sought advice from his insurance company about the financial soundness of an associated company. On the basis of the information he was given not only did he keep his investment in the company but he invested more money. The insurance company had given him false information and he suffered financial loss.

HELD: The Privy Council took a narrow approach to the requirement for special skill on the part of the defendant. The majority held that the insurance company was not in the business of giving advice about investments and that the duty only arose when the defendant was in the business of giving the advice in question or had held himself out as competent to do so. [1971] A.C. 793

COMMENTARY

Lords Reid and Morris dissenting, expressed the opinion that it was sufficient that considered advice was sought from a businessman in the course of his business. In subsequent decisions the minority view, that the "special relationship" could include any business or professional relationship has gained acceptance. For example, in *Esso Petroleum Ltd v. Mardon* [1976] 1 Q.B. 801, the Court of Appeal held that although the defendants were not in the business of giving advice they had special knowledge and skill in estimating the petrol throughput at a filling station, whereas the plaintiff did not.

Key Principle: A gratuitous agent might owe a duty of care where the circumstances make it clear that considered advice is being sought.

Chaudry v. Prabhakar 1989

The plaintiff asked a friend who had some knowledge of cars, though not a mechanic, to find a suitable car that had not been involved in an accident. The defendant found her a car which he recommended but which was subsequently discovered to have been involved in a serious accident, poorly repaired and unroadworthy. [1989] 1 W.L.R. 29

HELD: The Court of Appeal imposed liability on the defendant but Stocker L.J. stated that: "in the absence of other factors giving rise to such a duty, the giving of advice sought in the context of family, domestic or social relationships will not in itself give rise to any duty in respect of such advice." In such situations there would not be reasonable reliance.

Key Principle: Liability will arise where the defendant has known, or have been in such a position to reasonably be expected to have known, that the plaintiff would rely on the statement, and the plaintiff's reliance on the statement must have been reasonable.

Smith v. Bush 1990

The plaintiff purchaser was required to pay for a surveyor's valuation for the purpose of a mortgage application. The defendant surveyor was acting for the building society mortgagees to enable them to decide if the property provided adequate security for the loan. The plaintiff, to her detriment, relied on the valuation.

HELD: The plaintiff succeeded. The surveyor, acting for the building society, owed a duty of care to the intending purchaser who, as he knew, would rely upon his skill without obtaining an independent survey. [1990] 1 A.C. 831

COMMENTARY
(1) In this case the fact that the size of the house price was relatively small when compared with the cost of commissioning an independent survey was an important factor in categorising the plaintiff's reliance as reasonable. However, it may not be reasonable for all purchasers to rely on the mortgagee's valuer (for example, very expensive houses or commercial property).
(2) The impact of the *Unfair Contract Terms Act 1977* can be seen in both this case, and in *Harris v. Wyre Forest District Council* [1990] 1 A.C. 831, concerning a survey which had been carried out by a local authority surveyor. In both cases disclaimer clauses which had been inserted in the valuations were struck down by the House of Lords as unreasonable under the Act.

Key Principle: For liability to arise:

(i)   the loss must be reasonably foreseeable;

(ii)   there must be a relationship of proximity between the parties; and

(iii)   it must be fair, just and reasonable that the law should impose a duty.

Caparo Industries plc v. Dickman 1990
The plaintiffs owned shares in a public company whose accounts were audited by the defendants for the purposes of the annual statutory audit. The plaintiffs purchased further shares and made a successful takeover bid for the company. They subsequently suffered a substantial loss and brought an action against the auditors. It was alleged that the shares had been purchased in reliance on the audit which was negligently prepared and gave a misleading impression of the company's financial position.
HELD: (HL) The plaintiff's claim failed. The auditors owed no duty of care in respect of the accuracy of the accounts to either members of the public or existing shareholders when they rely on such an audit to invest in the company: there was not sufficient proximity between the plaintiffs and the defendants. Also, the audit was prepared for the purpose of enabling the shareholders as a body to exercise control over the company: it was not prepared for the purpose of providing information for investors. [1990] 2 A.C. 605

COMMENTARY
(1) In this case the statement was placed into general circulation as opposed to the "one to one" situations in *Hedley Byrne* and *Smith v. Bush*. Lord Bridge said that an essential ingredient of the required proximity in situations where a statement is put into more or less general circulation is to prove that:

> "the defendant knew that his statement would be communicated to the plaintiff, either as an individual or as a member of an identifiable class, specifically in connection with a particular transaction or transactions of a particular kind, . . . and that the plaintiff would be very likely to rely on it . . ."

(2) This restricted approach to liability was applied in *Al-Nakib Investments (Jersey) Ltd v. Longcroft* [1990] 3 All E.R. 321, where directors issued a prospectus inviting shareholders to subscribe for additional shares in the company. The purpose of the prospectus was specifically to invite existing shareholders to apply and a claim brought by purchasers in the market was struck out.

Key Principle: Where express representations are made on a business occasion the form in which the information is given may negative the existence of a duty of care.

James McNaughton Paper Group Ltd v. Hicks Anderson & Co. 1991
The defendant accountants became aware that the plaintiffs were considering a takeover of their clients, M.K. At a meeting between the two companies the defendants were asked to confirm the accuracy of the draft accounts which they had prepared for M.K.'s chairman to be used in the negotiations. They responded in a general way that M.K. was breaking even or doing marginally worse. After the takeover the plaintiffs discovered discrepancies in the accounts and sued the defendant accountants.
HELD: (CA) The defendants owed no duty of care to the plaintiffs because the accounts were prepared for M.K. and not the plaintiffs. The plaintiff as buyers were aware of the poor state of M.K.'s affairs and could be expected to consult their own accountants. [1991] 2 Q.B. 113

COMMENTARY

(1) Neil L.J., accepting that there could be considerable overlap, made an analysis of the relevant cases and identified criteria which might be applied in determining the existence of a duty of care following *Caparo*:

(i)   the purpose for which the statement was made;

(ii) the purpose for which the statement was communicated;

(iii) the relationship between the adviser, advisee and any third party;

(iv) the size of any class to which the advisee belongs;

(v)   the state of knowledge of the adviser; and

(vi) reliance by the advisee.

(2) In *Morgan Crucible Co. plc v. Hill Samuel Bank Ltd* [1991] 1 All E.R. 148, the defendants who had prepared profit forecasts expressly designed to induce the plaintiffs to bid for a company in a contested takeover were found to owe a duty of care. *Caparo* was distinguished on the ground that the representations were made after, not before the identified bidder had emerged and the representations were made in the knowledge and with the intention that they should be relied on.

Variations on Hedley Byrne

Key Principle: Reliance on the statement by the plaintiff is not essential to establish a duty of care; the assumption of responsibility by a solicitor towards a client extends to the intended beneficiary.

White v. Jones 1995
The plaintiffs were disinherited by their father in his will after a family row in 1986. Six months later a reconciliation took place and in July 1986 the father gave his solicitors instructions to draw up a new will giving his daughters £9,000 each. The solicitors delayed in carrying out the father's request and after a month he renewed his instructions. The solicitors still failed to act by the time the father, who was 78, died in September 1986.
HELD: A remedy under the *Hedley Byrne* principle was extended and the sisters were entitled to recover damages from the defendants in negligence. [1995] 1 All E.R. 691

COMMENTARY

The House stated that by accepting instructions to draw up a will, a solicitor came into a "special relationship with those intended to benefit under it" and this, in consequence, imposed a duty on the solicitor to "act with due expedition and care" on behalf of the beneficiaries. This decision re-affirmed *Ross v. Caunters* [1980] Ch. 297, a first instance decision, where the defendant solicitor had failed to warn the testator that the will should not be witnessed by the husband of the intended beneficiary. When the disappointed beneficiary under the ineffective will sued the solicitors they admitted negligence but argued that the only duty they owed was to the testator. But Megarry V.-C. held that a duty of care was owed to the plaintiff as a sufficient relationship of neighbourhood or proximity existed between the parties.

Key Principle: A party who negligently supplies a defamatory reference about a person in response to a request from a potential employer may be liable in negligence to the subject of the reference.

Spring v. Guardian Assurance 1994

The plaintiff was dismissed from his job by the defendant and attempted to set up his own business selling life assurance policies on behalf of other companies. Before he could start work, regulations relating to the financial services industry required the defendant to provide a reference. The defendant supplied a damning reference which mistakenly alleged that the plaintiff was dishonest. As a consequence the plaintiff's business failed. Even though the reference was defamatory the plaintiff would not have succeeded in an action for defamation. Since, in the absence of malice, the defendant would have been able to establish a defence of qualified privilege. The plaintiff instead sued in negligence. The defendant argued:

(i) to give a cause of action in negligence would distort and subvert the tort of defamation and;

(ii) if the plaintiff won, employers fearful of liability, would be involuntary to write references or supply only bland references that conveyed no relevant information.

HELD: In holding the defendant liable, the majority in the House of Lords agreed that the preservation of the law of defamation would not be sufficient to deny the plaintiff a remedy. [1994] 3 All E.R. 129

COMMENTARY

The majority (Lord Keith dissenting) decided that the two torts were different. Defamation exists to protect reputation but a negligent reference can do harm without affecting a person's reputation. This decision approves *Lawton v. B.O.C. Transhield Ltd* [1987] 2 All E.R. 608 where it was held that a duty could be owed, at least to check the facts upon which the statement was made were accurate, by an employer who gives a negligent reference about an employee. Both this case and *White v. Jones* (above), endorsing the wider interpretation of *Hedley Byrne*, mark a reversal of the trend to restrict the development of negligence.

7. DEFENCES TO NEGLIGENCE

Not all possible defences in tort actions are discussed here. Some defences are specific to particular torts—for example, justification in defamation—and are considered with those torts. This chapter is concerned with defences which have a particular relevance to claims in negligence. The first of these, contributory negligence, operates where the plaintiff's own fault has contributed to the damage suffered and the damages payable are reduced in proportion to the degree of fault. The second defence is *volenti non fit injuria*—no wrong is done to one who consents. This means that a plaintiff who voluntarily agrees to undertake the risk of harm is not permitted to sue for the consequent damage. It is a complete defence and if it succeeds the plaintiff gets nothing. The third defence of *ex turpi causa non oritur actio*—no right of action arises from a bad cause—means that a defendant is not liable for damage in circumstances where the plaintiff was participating in an unlawful act.

Contributory Negligence

Before the Law Reform (Contributory Negligence) Act 1945, contributory negligence was a complete defence and no damages were recoverable where injuries were caused partly by the plaintiff's own fault. Under the Act, section 1(1) the court has power to apportion the damage and, where a plaintiff's own conduct has contributed to the accident or harm, to reduce the damages awarded. In *Pitts v. Hunt* [1991] 1 Q.B. 24 the Court of Appeal announced that for the Act to come into operation there must be fault on the part of both parties. A finding that the plaintiff was 100 per cent contributory negligent was not allowed on the basis that holding the plaintiff entirely at fault would effectively defeat his claim.

Key Principle: The plaintiff's carelessness need not be a cause of the accident but it is essential to show that it contributed to the damage suffered.

Froom v. Butcher 1976
The plaintiff was involved in a collision caused by the defendant's negligence. He was not wearing a seat belt but if he had been wearing a belt the head and chest injuries which he sustained in the accident would have been avoided.
HELD: (CA) The standard of care is objective. In failing to wear a seat belt the plaintiff failed to take reasonable precautions for his own safety and his damages were reduced accordingly. [1976] 2 Q.B. 286

COMMENTARY
(1) The negligence of the plaintiff did not contribute to the accident happening, but his failure to take precautions increased the risk of harm.
(2) In this case the plaintiff had made a conscious decision not to wear the seat belt because of the risk of becoming trapped in an accident. However, in *Condon v. Condon* [1978] R.T.R. 483 a plaintiff who claimed to suffer from a seat-belt phobia was not held to be contributorily negligent for failing to do so.

Key Principle: **Accepting a lift from a driver whom the plaintiff knows has consumed large quantities of alcohol may amount to contributory negligence.**

Owens v. Brimmell 1977

The plaintiff and the defendant went on a pub-crawl together and each consumed about eight or nine pints of beer. On the journey home the defendant negligently drove into a lamp post.

HELD: The plaintiff was 20 per cent contributorily negligent in getting into the car with a driver whom he knew to be drunk, even if at the time he himself was too drunk to know how drunk the driver was. [1977] Q.B. 859

Key Principle: **The injury sustained must be within the scope of the risk created by the plaintiff's negligence.**

Jones v. Livox Quarries Ltd 1952

The plaintiff, disregarding his employer's safety instructions, was riding on the towbar of a traxcavator when another employee negligently drove into the back of the vehicle and caused him injury. The plaintiff argued that his contributory negligence should not count against him because the obvious danger arising from riding on the towbar was being thrown off, not being run into from behind and crushed by another vehicle.

HELD: (CA) The risk of being run into from behind was also one to which the plaintiff had exposed himself and his damages were reduced accordingly. [1952] 2 Q.B. 608

COMMENTARY

Lord Denning said that the plaintiff's carelessness would have been irrelevant if, instead of being hit by another vehicle, he had been struck in the eye by a shot fired by a negligent sportsman.

Key Principle: In the case of children, age is a circumstance which must be considered in deciding if there has been contributory negligence.

Yachuk v. Oliver Blais Co. Ltd 1949
The defendants supplied a nine-year old boy with a pint of petrol. He had falsely stated that his mother wanted the petrol for her car. When he used the fuel to make a burning torch for the purposes of a game he suffered severe injury.
HELD: The defendants were liable in negligence for supplying petrol to so young a boy. He had not been guilty of contributory negligence for he neither knew nor could be expected to know of the danger. [1949] A.C. 386

COMMENTARY
(1) In *Gough v. Thorne* [1966] 3 All E.R. 398, the plaintiff, a 13-year-old girl, was waiting to cross the road. She was beckoned to proceed by the driver of a lorry and as she did so she was struck by the defendant who was driving too fast. The fact that she had relied entirely on the driver's signal to cross the road did not constitute contributory negligence. According to Lord Denning: "A very young child cannot be guilty of contributory negligence."
(2) Where an employee is suing an employer the courts are reluctant to make a finding of contributory negligence. In *Caswell v. Powell Duffryn Associated Collieries* [1940] A.C. 152, it was held that regard must be had to the dulling of the sense of danger through familiarity, repetition, noise, confusion, fatigue and preoccupation with work.

Key Principle: Where a defendant's negligence creates an emergency the court is reluctant to find contributory negligence on the part of a plaintiff who makes a wrong decision in the agony of the moment.

Jones v. Boyce 1816
The plaintiff was a passenger on the defendant's coach and, fearing that it was about to overturn, he jumped off. The coach did not overturn and had he stayed where he was the plaintiff would have been safe.
HELD: He was not guilty of contributory negligence because he had acted reasonably in the circumstances. (1816) 1 Stark 493

Volenti non fit injuria

Key Principle: The defendant will not be liable if the plaintiff voluntarily assumed to take the risk involved—but knowledge of the danger does not necessarily imply consent.

Smith v. Charles Baker & Sons 1891

The plaintiff was employed drilling holes in a rock cutting over which a crane often swung heavy stones while he was working. He was aware that there was a risk of the stones falling and he had complained to his employer about the dangerous practice. When he was injured by a falling stone he brought an action against his employers, who pleaded *volenti non fit injuria*.

HELD: (HL) *Volenti* was rejected—even though the plaintiff had knowledge of the danger and continued to work, he had not voluntarily undertaken the risk. [1891] A.C. 325

COMMENTARY

(1) See also *Rathcliff v. McDonnell and Another* (1998) (see p. 122) where, knowing of the risk involved, the plaintiff was held to have willingly accepted the risk as his.

(2) The defence will rarely be successful in an action by an employee against an employer. However, it was accepted by the House of Lords in *Imperial Chemical Industries Ltd (I.C.I.) v. Shatwell* [1965] A.C. 656. The plaintiff, in defiance of his employer's orders and statutory safety regulations, went to test some detonators without taking the required safety precautions. During the testing an explosion occurred and the plaintiff was injured. His employer was not liable because the plaintiff was held to have consented to and fully appreciated the risk of injury.

Key Principle: In circumstance where the plaintiff accepts a lift from an obviously inebriated driver the plea of *volenti* depends on the degree of intoxication.

Morris v. Murray 1991

After a bout of heavy drinking Murray suggested to Morris that they go for a spin in his light aircraft. Soon after take-off the aircraft crashed killing Murray and severely injuring Morris who brought an action against the deceased's estate.

HELD: (CA) The defence succeeded on the ground that the pilot's drunkenness was so extreme and obvious that the plaintiff was *volens* to the risk. [1991] 2 Q.B. 6

COMMENTARY
In *Dann v. Hamilton* [1939] 1 K.B. 509, the defendant had driven the plaintiff and her mother to see the Coronation decorations. They visited several public houses and it became obvious that the defendant's ability to drive was impaired. But the plea of *volenti* was rejected and the plaintiff was found not to have consented to or absolved the defendant from subsequent negligence on his part. Asquith J. held that *volenti* did not apply to this situation, unless the drunkeness was so extreme and so glaring that accepting a lift was equivalent to ". . . walking on the edge of an unfenced cliff". (*Volenti* is excluded by section 149 of the Road Traffic Act 1988, see *Pitts v. Hunt*, below).

Key Principle: The doctrine of the assumption of risk does not apply to a rescuer when the emergency was created by the defendant's negligence.

Baker v. Hopkins 1959
The defendant employer had adopted a dangerous system of working by lowering a petrol engine down into the inside of a well. The engine discharged poisonous emissions and two of the workmen were overcome by the fumes. The plaintiff, a doctor, had volunteered to go down the well to rescue the workmen. He too was overcome by the fumes and was killed.
HELD: (CA) *Volenti* was inapplicable because the plaintiff's actions as a rescuer were not truly voluntary. This decision can also be explained on policy grounds as it is against the public interest to deter rescue. [1959] 3 All E.R. 225

COMMENTARY
If there is no genuine emergency the plaintiff might be *volens*. In *Cutler v. United Dairies Ltd* [1933] 2 K.B. 197 the plaintiff was *volens* because there was nobody in danger when he tried to calm a horse which had bolted into a field.

Ex turpi causa non oritur actio

Key Principle: **The courts will not assist a plaintiff who has been guilty of illegal conduct.**

Pitts v. Hunt 1990
On their way back from a disco at which they had both consumed large amounts of alcohol, the plaintiff encouraged the defendant to drive his motorbike in a reckless and dangerous fashion. The defendant was killed and the plaintiff, who was a pillion passenger, was badly injured.
HELD: (CA) The defendant's own criminal and disgraceful conduct gave rise to a successful defence of the *ex turpi causa.* [1991] 1 Q.B. 24

COMMENTARY
(1) The court concluded that the defence of *volenti non fit injuria* which was also raised, is excluded under the Road Traffic Act 1988 in circumstances where insurance is compulsory (as it is with motor insurance).
(2) In *Clunis v. Camden and Islington Health Authority* [1998] 3 All E.R. 180 the plaintiff, who had a history of mental illness, killed a stranger in a violent attack. Before he killed the victim he had been discharged into the care of the defendant health authority. He claimed that they were negligent in failing to treat him with reasonable care and skill. In holding that the maxim *ex turpo causa non oritur actio* applied, the Court of Appeal said that a plaintiff who had been convicted of a serious offence could not, on the ground of public policy, sue a health authority in negligence in failing to treat him properly thereby preventing him from committing the offence.

8. EMPLOYERS' LIABILITY AT COMMON LAW

The liability of an employer to an employee has two aspects. The first, liability for harm caused by employees in the course of their employment—vicarious liability—is dealt with in Chapter 2. The second, liability to employees in respect of harm suffered at work, is the subject of this chapter. In *Priestly v. Fowler* (1837) 3 M. & W. 1 it was decided that an employer would not be vicariously liable for harm inflicted on workers by fellow employees. This was known as the doctrine of "common employment" and the theory was that the contract of employment contained an implied term that an employee agreed to accept the risks incidental to the employment, including the risk of negligence of fellow employees. Where a risk had been created by the employer the defence of *volenti non fit injuria*, which was a complete defence until the Law Reform Contributory Negligence Act 1945, could usually be established by the employer. These two defences together with the defence of contributory negligence were known as the "unholy trinity" and combined they prevented virtually any action in tort by employees. As judicial attitudes began to change the law developed techniques to mitigate the harshness of the rule, in *Smith v. Charles Baker & Sons* (1891) (see p. 79) the House of Lords made it difficult for employers to establish the defence of *volenti*. In *Wilson and Clyde Coal v. English* (1938) (see below) it was held that an employer owed a personal and non-delegable duty to an employee and where the employer was in breach of this duty the defence of common employment could not be relied on. The employer's duty is a general duty to take reasonable care for the physical safety of the employee, it does not extend to protecting the employee's economic welfare. In *Reid v. Rush and Tompkins Group plc* [1989] 3 All E.R. 228, it was held that an employer had no duty to arrange accident insurance for a person working abroad or to warn the employee of the need to take out such insurance.

Key Principle: **The employer's obligation for the employee's safety is fulfilled by due care and skill. But it is not fulfilled by delegation to employees, even though selected with due care and skill.**

Wilson and Clyde Coal Co. v. English 1938

The plaintiff miner was injured at the defendant's coal mine. He was travelling through the pit at the end of a day shift and was crushed when the haulage plant was set in motion. The haulage equipment should have been stopped during travelling time. The defendant employers claimed that they had discharged their duty of providing a safe system of work by appointing a competent and qualified manager.

HELD: (HL) The employers were liable. They could not avoid their duty to provide a reasonably safe system of working by delegation to a competent employee. [1938] A.C. 57

COMMENTARY

The employer's duty, which was stated to be "the provision of a competent staff of men, adequate material and a proper system and effective supervision", is commonly analysed in four elements. The following cases are grouped to reflect this approach.

Competent Staff

Key Principle: The employer owes a duty to employees to select competent employees and to give them proper instructions and supervision.

General Cleaning Contractors v. Christmas 1953

A window cleaner was sent to clean the windows of a club. He was instructed by his employers in the sill method of cleaning windows and while he was holding on to one window-sash for support the window came down on his fingers causing him to fall to the ground.

HELD: (HL) The employers were liable, the plaintiff should have been given proper instruction and told to test the sashes. [1953] A.C. 180

COMMENTARY

This duty to select competent employees is of little importance since the abolition of the doctrine of common employment because the employer will be vicariously liable for the tort of one employee against another. However, it can be relevant. It is unlikely that an employer will be vicariously liable where one employee is injured by an attack or violent horseplay of another. In *Hudson v. Ridge Manufacturing Co. Ltd* [1957] 2 Q.B. 348, an employee was injured by a practical joker who had a reputation for persistently engaging in practical jokes. The employer was liable for breach of his personal duty because he should have known about and taken steps to deal with the jester.

Safe Place of Work

Key Principle: The employer must provide a safe place of work, but this duty is discharged if the employer takes reasonable steps to see that the premises are safe.

Latimer v. A.E.C. Ltd 1953

The defendants' large factory was flooded after a heavy rainfall and the water mixed with an oily liquid which usually collected in channels in the floor. When the mixture drained away it left the floor very slippery. Sawdust was spread over most, but not all, of the surface. A workman was injured when he slipped on the untreated part of the floor. The trial judge had found the defendants liable on the ground that they had not closed down the factory.

HELD: (HL) Allowing the appeal, it was held that the defendants were not liable: they had acted as a reasonable employer would have acted. The danger was not such as to impose on the employer an obligation to close down the factory. [1953] 2 All E.R. 499

Proper Plant and Equipment

Key Principle: At common law an employer was not liable for the defects in the manufacture of a tool which could not have been discovered with reasonable inspection.

Davie v. New Merton Board Mills 1959

The plaintiff employee was blinded when a particle of metal chipped off the tool with which he was working. The tool had been negligently manufactured but outwardly it appeared to be in good condition.

HELD: The employer had bought the tool from a reputable manufacturer and had therefore discharged his duty to the employee. [1959] A.C. 604

COMMENTARY

The effect of this decision was to leave the injured employee without compensation where the manufacturer or supplier could not be found or who was bankrupt. The decision has been reversed by the Employers' Liability (Defective Equipment) Act 1969 which makes the employer liable where an employee is injured in the course of employment by defective equipment.

Key Principle: **The Employers' Liability (Defective Equipment) Act 1969 covers defective plant of every sort with which the employee is compelled to work.**

Coltman v. Bibby Tankers 1988

This case arose out of the sinking of *The Derbyshire* with the loss of all hands off the coast of Japan in 1980. The plaintiffs, personal representatives of a crew member, alleged that due to the manufacturers negligence the ship was defectively constructed. They claimed that these were defects in equipment and argued that the ship was "equipment" within section 1 of the Employers' Liability (Defective Equipment) Act 1969.

HELD: The meaning of the word "equipment" can include ships or vessels for the purposes of the Act. [1988] A.C. 276

COMMENTARY

Equipment is given a broad interpretation and in *Knowles v. Liverpool City Council* [1993] 1 W.L.R. 1428 was found to include a flagstone being laid by a council workman.

Safe System of Work

Key Principle: **The duty will normally apply in a system of working which is regular or routine and includes: the physical lay-out of the job; the sequence in which the work is to be carried out; the provision in appropriate cases of warnings and notices; and the issue of special instructions.**

Speed v. Thomas Swift and Co. Ltd 1943

The plaintiff was loading a ship from a barge, an operation which was normally carried out while the ship's rails were left in position. Sections of the rail had been damaged and the resulting circumstances made it unsafe on the occasion in question to load the ship. As a result the plaintiff was injured.

HELD: The employers were liable because in the circumstances they had not laid out a safe system of work. [1943] K.B. 557

COMMENTARY
The general practice of a particular trade will be relevant in deciding whether or not the duty has been breached, but in *General Cleaning Contractors v. Christmas* (see p. 83) the House of Lords said that where a practice of ignoring an obvious danger has evolved it is not reasonable to expect an individual workman to devise precautions.

Key Principle: The concept of a safe system of work contemplates that an employee should not suffer stress as a result of certain forms of behaviour by the employer.

Walker v. Northumberland County Council 1995
The plaintiff, an area social services officer, having suffered two mental breakdowns was dismissed on grounds of ill-health. He alleged that his ill health was caused by the stress of his work and claimed damages from his employers.
HELD: The employers were liable. The employer's duty extends to protection against psychiatric harm in circumstances where this type of damage is foreseeable. [1995] I.R.L.R. 35

COMMENTARY
In *Johnstone v. Bloomsbury Area Health Authority* [1992] 1 Q.B. 333, the Court of Appeal held that the employers could not lawfully require a junior doctor to work so much overtime as was reasonably foreseeable would damage his health.

Key Principle: Employers must warn employees of any inherent dangers in the work which they are required to do.

Pape v. Cumbria County Council 1992
The plaintiff was a part-time cleaner employed by the defendants. She was required to use various detergents and chemical cleaning products in the course of her work. Although the defendants had provided gloves they did not warn her of the danger of contracting dermatitis or instruct her to wear the gloves. When the plaintiff developed dermatitis she sued the employers.
HELD: The employers were liable: they had failed to provide a safe system of work in not warning the plaintiff of the dangers of contracting dermatitis if the gloves were not worn. [1992] I.C.R. 132

Employer's Indemnity

Key Principle: An employer who has been held vicariously liable for an employee's negligence is entitled to seek an indemnity from the employee to recover any damages paid.

Lister v. Romford Ice & Cold Storage Co. 1957

Lister was employed as a lorry driver. In the course of his employment he was driving negligently when he injured his father, a fellow employee. The employers were vicariously liable and the father's damages were paid by the employers' insurers. Exercising their right of subrogation the insurers then brought an action against the son for an indemnity.

HELD: (HL) The son was liable to indemnify the employers, and hence the insurers. [1957] A.C. 555

COMMENTARY
(1) It must be noted that the employer it is liable as well as the employee. As joint tort-feasors they are each fully liable to the plaintiff.
(2) Because of the problems predicted for industrial relations following this decision the employers' liability insurers entered into a "gentleman's agreement" not to take advantage of this principle unless there was evidence of collusion or misconduct.

9. PRODUCT LIABILITY

In addition to rights under the common law, with which the cases in this chapter are concerned, there is an additional form of liability for defective products. The Consumer Protection Act 1987 imposes strict liability for defective products which cause personal injury and damage to private property. The most notable feature of the Act is that it removes the need for those injured by a product to establish fault on the part of the producer, but it is also important to note that the Act has not replaced the common law. The Act only applies to "producers" and where, for example, an

injury is caused by a defectively repaired product, a plaintiff
will need to rely on the common law. The Act does not apply
to injuries caused by unprocessed agricultural products or
where there is damage to goods used for commercial purposes. Also, where the special limitation periods under the
Act have expired a claim in negligence may still be available.

Key Principle: **Even in the absence of a contract a manufacturer
can be liable to the ultimate consumer where a product has caused
physical damage.**

Donoghue v. Stevenson 1932
As a consequence of drinking ginger beer from an opaque bottle
which allegedly included the remains of a decomposed snail, the
plaintiff became ill. Because the drink had been bought for her by
a friend, there was no contractual duty between the plaintiff and
the manufacturer of the ginger beer.
HELD: (HL) The Court rejected the privity defence and found
the manufacturers liable. [1932] A.C. 562

COMMENTARY
(1) The element of this decision which provided the foundations for a general duty of care in negligence is known as the
wide ratio. But the case actually concerned liability for
defective products which caused harm and this specific
duty expressed by Lord Atkin is known as the *narrow ratio*:

> ". . . a manufacturer of products, which he sells in such a form
> as to show that he intends them to reach the ultimate consumer
> in the form in which they left him with no reasonable possibility
> of intermediate examination and with the knowledge that the
> absence of reasonable care in the preparation or putting up of
> the products will result in an injury to the consumer's life or
> property, owes a duty to the consumer to take reasonable care."

In the cases below *each of the elements* of the narrow ratio
will be considered in turn.
(2) Generally speaking, there is no tort action where a product is merely defective and has not caused any physical
damage. The law of contract provides the basis of protection
for products which are defective in quality, though not
dangerous.

Key Principle: A manufacturer has been given a wide interpretation by the courts and extended beyond the maker of a product. Mere distributors or suppliers and repairers of goods may incur liability.

Stennett v. Hancock and Peters 1939

The plaintiff pedestrian was injured when he was struck by a flange which had come off one of the wheels of the first defendant's lorry. The wheel had earlier been repaired by the second defendants and the cause of the accident was found to be the careless re-assembly of the wheel by one of the second defendant's employees.
HELD: The claim against the first defendant failed but the second defendant (the repairer) was held liable under the principle of *Donoghue v. Stevenson* [1939] 2 All E.R. 578

COMMENTARY

This principle has been extended to:

(i)   suppliers, liability can arise in circumstances where a supplier would normally be expected to check for safety before selling the goods. In *Andrews v. Hopkinson* [1957] 1 Q.B. 229, a second-hand car dealer was held liable because defective steering on an 18-year old car could easily have been discovered by a competent mechanic;

(ii)   distributors, in *Watson v. Buckley, Osborne, Garrett & Co.* [1940] 1 All E.R. 174, the distributors who failed to test a hair dye for themselves before they advertised it as harmless were held to be negligent.

Key Principle: The definition of a product has been extended beyond food and drink to include all manufactured products capable of causing damage.

Grant v. Australian Knitting Mills Ltd 1936

The plaintiff contracted dermatitis through wearing woollen underpants which had been manufactured by the defendants. The disease was caused by invisible excess sulphites which had been negligently left in the underwear during the manufacturing process. The defendant contended that *Donoghue v. Stevenson* could be distinguished on the ground that the ginger beer was to be

consumed internally whereas the underpants were to be worn externally.
HELD: (PC) The defendants were liable. No distinction can be logically drawn between a noxious thing taken internally and a noxious thing applied externally. [1936] A.C. 85

COMMENTARY
In *Haseldine v. C.A. Daw & Son Ltd* [1941] 2 K.B. 343, the definition of a product was extended to include a lift.

Key Principle: The *ultimate consumer* is construed very widely to include any user of the product and persons less obviously at risk may be within the scope of the manufacturer's duty.

Barnett v. H. and J. Packer & Co. 1940
The plaintiff, a shop-keeper, was injured by a piece of metal protruding from a sweet. He sued the defendant manufacturers.
HELD: The plaintiff was a "consumer" and as the manufacturer of the product the defendant was liable. [1940] 3 All E.R. 575

COMMENTARY
The expansion of the class of plaintiffs is illustrated by *Stennett v. Hancock and Peters* (see p. 89) where a pedestrian was held to be within the rule in *Donoghue v. Stevenson*.

Key Principle: No reasonable possibility of intermediate examination has been widely interpreted by the courts—a mere opportunity for intermediate examination will not exonerate the defendant—there must be a reasonable probability of intermediate inspection.

Griffiths v. Arch Engineering Co. 1968
The plaintiff was injured by a portable grinding tool which he borrowed from the first defendants but which was actually owned by the second defendants. It was lent by the first defendants without further inspection and without knowledge that it had been made dangerous by an employee of the second defendants.
HELD: The first defendants were liable because they had an opportunity to examine the tool and failed to do so. The second

defendants were equally liable because they had no reason to suppose that such an examination would be carried out. [1968] 3 All E.R. 217

COMMENTARY
A manufacturer who has no reason to believe that an intermediate inspection will take place, whether by a third party or the consumer, will be liable. The product need not reach the ultimate consumer in a sealed package for the duty to arise, in *Grant v. Australian Knitting Mills* (see p. 89) the Privy Council stated that for the rule to apply "the customer must use the article exactly as it left the maker, that is in all material features, and use it as it was intended to be used."

Key Principle: **The plaintiff will generally discharge the burden of proof by showing the existence of the defect and that on the balance of probabilities it arose in the course of manufacture.**

Mason v. Williams & Williams Ltd 1955
While using a cold chisel which was too hard for its purpose the plaintiff suffered an eye injury and had to have his eye removed. The chisel had been supplied by the first defendants, the employers, and manufactured by the second defendants. There was no suggestion that the plaintiff had been at fault in using the chisel, and it had only been taken out of the stores a few weeks beforehand.
HELD: Since the plaintiff had established that nothing had happened to the chisel after it had left the defendant manufacturer's factory which could have caused the excessive hardness their negligence was established. [1955] 1 W.L.R. 549

COMMENTARY
In *Carroll v. Fearon, The Times,* January 26, 1998, a serious accident occurred when a car went out of control and crashed into an oncoming vehicle. The cause of the accident was a sudden and complete thread strip of a rear tyre. The Court of Appeal found that there was overwhelming evidence of a defective manufacturing process and held that there was no requirement to identify any particular individual as being responsible for the defect, nor any need for the particular aspect of negligence to be specified.

Key Principle: In order to establish liability there must be sufficient evidence that the defect existed in the product when it left the manufacturer.

Evans v. Triplex Safety Glass Co. Ltd 1936
The plaintiff bought a Vauxhall car fitted with a windscreen made of "Triplex Toughened Safety Glass". A year later when he was driving the car, with his wife and son as passengers, the windscreen suddenly and for no apparent reason cracked and disintegrated. The occupants of the car were injured and brought an action against the manufacturers of the windscreen.
HELD: The defendants were not liable. The windscreen might have been interfered with and the defect introduced by any one of a range of alternative causes other than a defect in manufacture. Relevant factors were the lapse of time between the purchase of the windscreen and the accident and the possibility that the glass may have been strained when screwed into its frame. [1936] 1 All E.R. 283

Key Principle: A warning of danger, provided it is adequate in the circumstances, may absolve the defendant.

Kubach v. Hollands 1937
A manufacturer sold a chemical to the second defendants (retailers) and an accompanying invoice expressly stated, *inter alia*, that the chemical must be "examined and tested by user before use". The retailer failed to observe the manufacturer's instructions to test the product before labelling it and sold it to a science teacher. The chemical was used in a school experiment and it exploded, injuring and a schoolgirl and her father.
HELD: The retailer was liable but the manufacturers were not. They had given an adequate warning and the retailer had ignored it. [1937] 3 All E.R. 907

Key Principle: Knowledge of the risk will be irrelevant if there were no practical steps that the plaintiff could take to avoid the danger.

Denny v. Supplies and Transport Co. 1950
The plaintiff, in the course of his employment, was injured while he was unloading a barge of badly stowed timber. The plaintiff had complained to the wharf superintendent that the barge was badly loaded. Even though he realised that danger was imminent, it was shown that there is no safe way of unloading badly stowed timber.
HELD: (CA) The defendants were liable. The plaintiff had "no practical alternative to the course of conduct adopted." [1950] 2 K.B. 374

COMMENTARY
This case can be distinguished from *Farr v. Butters Bros* [1932] 2 K.B. 606 where there was no evidence of any legal or economic obligation on the plaintiff. The defendant crane manufacturers sent out a crane in parts to be assembled by the buyers. An experienced foreman realised the crane was defective but nevertheless ignored the danger and assembled it. The defendants were not liable when he was killed while working the crane on the grounds that the foreman had deliberately incurred the risk.

Key Principle: Liability for defective products is limited to personal injuries and physical damage to property other than the product itself.

Aswan Engineering Establishment Co. v. Lupdine Ltd 1987
The plaintiffs, a construction company, bought a quantity of waterproofing compound called Lupguard from the first defendants. The Lupguard was packed in heavy duty plastic pails manufactured by the second defendants. The pails containing the Lupguard were shipped to Kuwait where they were stacked on the quayside. Because of the high temperatures to which they were exposed the pails collapsed and much of the Lupguard was lost. The action failed in contract because the pails were of merchantable quality and there was no liability in tort because the damage was outside the range of what was reasonably foreseeable. One issue was whether the product had merely damaged itself or

whether the Lupguard was "other property" separate from the
pails.

HELD: (CA) Lloyd L.J. with whom Fox L.J. agreed expressed the
provisional view that the contents of the pails was "other property". Nicholls L.J. accepted that in strict legal analysis the
Lupguard and the pails were different property. However, he was
unhappy with the idea that the manufacturer of a container could
be liable under *Donoghue v. Stevenson* for loss of the contents due to a
defect in the container. [1987] 1 All E.R. 135

COMMENTARY
In *D. & F. Estates Ltd v. Church Commissioners* [1989] A.C.
177 Lord Bridge had advanced the "complex theory structure"—in a complex structure or complex chattels one part
of a structure or chattel might, when it caused damage to
another part of the structure or chattel, be regarded in tort
as having caused damage to "other property" for the
application of the *Donoghue v. Stevenson* principles. But
in *Murphy v. Brentwood District Council* (see p. 26) where
the foundations of the house subsided causing cracks in the
walls, the House of Lords made it clear that the cracks in the
walls constituted damage to the very property in question: it
was not a case of the defective foundations causing damage
to "other property".

The Consumer Protection Act 1987

The Consumer Protection Act 1987 provides a further possible
basis of claim. The Act creates strict liability on the producer of a
product which is *defective* and causes *personal injury* and, in
certain circumstances, *property damage*. The most notable feature
of the Act is that the plaintiff does not have to show fault on the
part of the producer but the Act does provide a number of
defences to the producer, the most important and controversial
of which is the development risks defence. The Act does not cover:
damage to the product itself; damage to property which is not
ordinarily intended for private use—there is no liability for
damage to business property; and damage where the amount of
the loss is less than £275. The exclusion of liability is prohibited
under the Act and in all cases there is a ten year limitation period
for bringing an action.

10. DEFAMATION

Libel—Slander

Key Principle: Libel is a defamatory statement which is conveyed in a permanent form.

Monson v. Tussauds 1894

The plaintiff had been tried for murder in Scotland and had argued successfully that the victim was killed by the accidental discharge of his own gun. The jury returned a verdict of not proven. Shortly after the trial, the defendants placed a model of the plaintiff and his gun in their exhibition of wax figures in a room which gave access to the Chamber of Horrors. The plaintiff applied for an interlocutory injunction to restrain the display of the wax figure until the trial of a libel action.

HELD: The injunction was not granted but the action was properly framed in libel. Lopes L.J. stated that

> ". . . Libels are generally in writing or printing, but this is not
> necessary; the defamatory matter may be conveyed in some
> other permanent form. For instance, a statute, a caricature,
> an effigy, chalk marks on a wall, signs or pictures may constitute
> a libel." [1894] 1 Q.B. 671

COMMENTARY

(1) Libel—defamatory material in a permanent form—should be distinguished from slander which takes a transient form: for example, spoken words, gestures, or mimicry.

(2) Libel is actionable *per se* but to succeed in an action for slander damage must be proved. However, there are four exceptional cases where slander is actionable *per se*:

(i)   imputation of crime. In *Webb v. Beavan* (1883) 11 Q.B.D. 606 the statement "I know enough to put you in goal" was actionable *per se*;

(ii)   words imputing that a person is suffering from a contagious disease, as in *Bloodworth v. Gray* (1844) 7 Man & G 334 "He has got that damned pox (meaning venereal disease) from going to that woman on the Derby Road";

(iii)   under the Slander of Women Act 1891, words
        imputing unchastity or adultery in any woman or
        girl. In *Youssoupoff v. Metro-Goldwyn-Mayer Pic-
        tures Ltd* (1934) 50 T.L.R. 581 a company was liable
        when a film about Rasputin suggested that the
        plaintiff had been seduced by him. It was held
        that a statement that a woman has been raped can
        affect her reputation;

(iv)   words calculated to disparage the plaintiff in any
        office, profession, trade or calling. In *Jones v. Jones*
        [1916] 2 A.C 481 an accusation that a schoolmaster
        had committed adultery with one of the school
        cleaners was not actionable *per se* (though an impu-
        tation of impropriety with a pupil might be).

Plaintiffs

Key Principle: A local authority or an organ of central government may not sue for defamation.

Derbyshire C.C. v. Times Newspapers Ltd 1993

The defendant had published articles questioning the propriety of
dealings in the plaintiff council's pension fund. The preliminary
point arose as to whether the plaintiff council could maintain an
action for libel.

HELD: (HL) A local authority cannot maintain an action for
libel on the ground that the threat of a civil action for defamation
would have an inhibiting effect on freedom of speech and it was
contrary to public interest that the organs of government, whether
central or local, should have a right to sue for libel. [1993] A.C.
534

COMMENTARY

(1) Individual councillors or officials may bring proceedings.
Lord Keith stated:

> "If the reputation of any of these is wrongly impaired by the
> publication any of these can himself bring proceedings for
> defamation."

(2) Only living persons can sue or defend an action in
defamation. However, in *Metropolitan Saloon Omnibus
Co. v. Hawkins* (1859) 4 H. & N. 87 insolvency was imputed
and it was held that where the statement affects its business

or property a trading corporation has a right to sue for defamation. But in *Electrical, Electronic, Telecommunication & Plumbing Union v. Times Newspapers* (1980) Q.B 585 it was held that trade unions, not being corporate bodies, lack the legal personality to sue.

A Defamatory Statement

Key Principle: Defamation is the publication of material which tends to lower the plaintiff in the estimation of right-thinking members of society generally.

Sim v. Stretch 1936
When Edith Saville, a maid who had left the plaintiff's employment, went to work for the defendant he sent a telegram to the plaintiff saying: "Edith has resumed service with us today. Please send her possessions and the money you borrowed also her wages to Old Barton. Sim." The plaintiff alleged that the telegram meant that he was in pecuniary difficulties and had to borrow money from his housemaid.
HELD: (HL) The words in question were not reasonably capable of a defamatory meaning. [1936] 2 All E.R. 1237

COMMENTARY
In *Parmiter v. Coupland* (1840) 6 M. & W. 105, Parke B. held a defamatory statement to be one "which is calculated to injure the reputation of another, by exposing him to hatred, contempt or ridicule." In *Youssoupoff* (see p. 96) Slesser L.J. expressed a defamatory statement to be one which tends to cause people to shun or avoid the plaintiff.

Key Principle: In defamation the test of what "right-thinking members of society" think appears to be determined by what they should think rather than what in fact they do think.

Byrne v. Deane 1937
A golf club had some gambling machines unlawfully kept in the club house. These were removed by police after somebody had informed of their illegal presence. Soon after this a verse appeared on the notice board of the club which ended with the lines: "But he who gave the game away, may he byrnne in hell and rue the day."

The plaintiff brought an action for libel alleging that by these words the defendants meant, and were understood to mean, that he was guilty of underhand disloyalty to his fellow members.

HELD: (CA) The plaintiff's claim failed. It could not be defamatory to "allege of a man . . . that he has reported certain acts, wrongful in law, to the police . . ." [1937] 1 K.B. 818

COMMENTARY

(1) In *Hartt v. Newspaper Publishing plc The Independent*, December 8, 1989, the Court of Appeal said the right-thinking person is not unduly suspicious but can read between the lines and engage in a certain amount of loose thinking, but is not avid for scandal, and will not select one bad meaning where other non-defamatory meanings are available.

(2) In *Gillick v. BBC, The Times*, October 20, 1995, it was held that words spoken in the course of a live television programme on the provision of contraceptive advice to young girls were capable of adversely affecting the plaintiff in the estimation of reasonable persons. In deciding whether the words were capable of bearing a defamatory meaning, they should be given the natural meaning which would be conveyed to an ordinary and reasonable hypothetical viewer watching the programme once, who was neither naïve nor unduly suspicious.

Key Principle: The statement must be understood by others to have a defamatory meaning.

Cassidy v. Daily Mirror Newspapers Ltd 1929

The defendants published a photograph of Mr Cassidy with a woman below which was carried an announcement of their engagement. The information on which the defendants based their statement came from Mr Cassidy alone and they had made no effort to verify it from any other source. Mr Cassidy was already married although he lived apart from his wife. However, he did occasionally stay with his wife at her flat. She brought an action in libel claiming that readers who knew her as Mr Cassidy's wife would assume that she had been lying about whether she was married to him.

HELD: The defendants were liable. The story would be understood by others to refer to the plaintiff and the newspaper's complete ignorance of the circumstances could not prevent the statement from having a defamatory meaning. [1929] 2 K.B. 331, CA

Innuendo

Key Principle: The plaintiff must rely on an innuendo where the words are not defamatory in their natural and ordinary meaning but may be defamatory when combined with extrinsic facts known to others about the situation.

Tolley v. J. S. Fry & Sons Ltd 1931
The defendants published an advertisement in which the plaintiff, a famous amateur golfer, was shown with a bar of Fry's chocolate in his back pocket and words which were understood to be his endorsement of the defendant's brand of chocolate. The defendants had not asked his permission to do this and the plaintiff alleged an innuendo that he had agreed to the advertisement for gain and had thus compromised his reputation as an amateur.
HELD: (HL) The advertisement was capable of bearing a defamatory meaning. [1930] 1 K.B. 467

COMMENTARY
(1) It is immaterial whether or not the defendant knows of the external facts which transform an innocent statement into a defamatory one, as in *Cassidy v. Daily Mirror* (see above) where the innuendo was that Mr Cassidy was not the plaintiff's husband but lived with her in immoral cohabitation.
(2) This type of innuendo, where the words are combined with extrinsic facts, is known as a "true" innuendo. It should be distinguished from a "false" innuendo where the defamatory implication is drawn from the words themselves, such as, for example, in *Allsop v. Church of England Newspapers Ltd* [1972] 2 Q.B. 161, where the defendant newspaper described a well-known broadcaster as "bent". The court said that in these circumstances the plaintiff must specify the slang meaning of the word relied on.

The Words Must Refer to the Plaintiff

Key Principle: The defendant's comment must be shown to refer to the plaintiff, but it need not be a specific reference. The test is to ask would ordinary sensible observers believe the plaintiff referred to.

Morgan v. Odhams Press Ltd 1971

The newspaper, *The Sun*, alleged that a girl had been kidnapped by a dog doping gang because she was threatening to inform the police of their activities. At the relevant time the girl had been staying at the plaintiff's flat and the plaintiff produced six witnesses who swore that they understood from the article that he was connected with the gang.

HELD: (HL) The story was capable of a defamatory meaning. There was no rule that the article should contain some kind of key or pointer to indicate the plaintiff, the question was whether readers who knew of the circumstances would reasonably have understood the article as referring to the plaintiff. [1971] 1 W.L.R. 1239

Key Principle: For liability to be imposed it is irrelevant that the defendant did not intend to refer to the plaintiff.

Hulton & Co. v. Jones 1910

The defendants published a humorous account of a motor festival at Dieppe which implied that a fictitious character "Armetus Jones", a churchwarden at Peckham, was behaving in a discreditable way with a woman in France. The plaintiff, a barrister who was not a churchwarden nor did he live in Peckham and did not visit the festival in Dieppe, sued for libel. Friends of his swore they believed that the article referred to him.

HELD: (HL) The defendants were liable. What mattered was how the words would be understood by others, not what they meant in the minds of the writer and the publisher. [1910] A.C. 20

COMMENTARY

(1) In *Newstead v. London Express Newspaper Ltd* [1940] 1 K.B. 377, the defendants were liable when the statement was true of one person and honestly intended for him but which could reasonably be attributed to the plaintiff. The statement that: "Harold Newstead, thirty-year old Camberwell

man" had been convicted of bigamy was true of a barman of that name but not of the plaintiff, Harold Newstead, an unmarried hairdresser from Camberwell aged about 30.

(2) These cases are now provided with the defence of "unintentional defamation" under section 4 of the Defamation Act 1952.

(3) The Defamation Act 1996 (ss. 2–4) has substantially changed the rules regulating unintentional defamation. The requirement of non-negligent innocence has been removed—the burden is on the *plaintiff* to show that the defendant had no reason to believe the statement referred to the plaintiff or that it was false and defamatory. The 1996 Act also permits a person who has published a statement alleged to be defamatory to make an offer of amends.

Key Principle: As a general rule, where a statement is directed to a class of persons no individual belonging to that class is entitled to sue unless:

(i) the class is so small that the statement must refer to each person in it; or

(ii) the words point to a particular plaintiff.

Knupffer v. London Express Newspapers Ltd 1944

The defendants published an article about a Young Russian political party which linked them with fascism. The party was an international organisation with a British branch consisting of 24 members. The plaintiff alleged that as the person responsible for the politics of the party the libel personally affected him.

HELD: (HL) That plaintiff's action failed. A general rule was laid down that where a class of persons is defamed it must be proved that the defamatory statement was capable of referring to the plaintiff and was in fact understood to do so. [1944] A.C. 116

Publication

Key Principle: There is publication where the statement is made known to a third party. This rule applies where the defendant knew or ought to have foreseen that the statement would come to the attention of a third party.

Huth v. Huth 1915

The defendant sent a letter in an unsealed envelope to the plaintiff which she alleged to be defamatory. The letter was opened and read by her inquisitive butler in an admitted breach of his duty. The plaintiff argued that since there was a presumption that postmen read postcards, even though they have no business doing so, the same presumption ought to apply to unsealed envelopes.

HELD: (CA) There was no publication even though the envelope was unsealed: it was not part of the butler's duty to open the letter and his conduct was not a direct consequence of sending it. [1915] 3 K.B. 32

Key Principle: There can be negligent publication if the reading of a letter is a natural and probable consequence of what the defendant did.

Theaker v. Richardson 1962

The defendant wrote a defamatory letter to the plaintiff, a married woman and a fellow member of the local district council. The letter was placed in a sealed envelope similar to those used for election addresses and sent to the plaintiff. Her husband opened the letter thinking it was an election address.

HELD: (CA) There was publication. A natural and probable consequence of the defendant's writing and delivery of the letter was that it would be opened and read by her husband. [1962] 1 W.L.R. 151

COMMENTARY

In *Wennhak v. Morgan* (1888) 20 Q.B.D. 635, it was held that making a statement to one's own spouse is not publication.

Key Principle: Every repetition of a defamatory statement is a fresh publication and creates a fresh cause of action against each successive publisher all the way down the chain of publication. However, those who are concerned with mere mechanical distribution of such matter, for example, newsagents, libraries and booksellers may have a defence of "innocent publication."

Vitzelli v. Mudie's Select Library 1900

The defendants, proprietors of a circulating library allowed people to use a book which, unknown to them, contained a libel on the plaintiff. In a publication taken by the defendants the publishers had circulated a notice requesting the return of copies of the offending book.

HELD: (CA) The defendants had failed to establish their "innocence" and were found liable. They had no procedure for checking whether their books contained libels and they had overlooked a publisher's request for the return of the particular book. [1900] 2 Q.B. 170

COMMENTARY
(1) The rule set out by Romer L.J. provides that mere mechanical distributors of such matter would have a defence if they could show that:

(i)   they were innocent of any knowledge of the libel in the work disseminated by them;

(ii)   there was no reason for them to be aware that the work contained a libel;

(iii) when the work was disseminated by them it was not by any negligence on their part that they did not know it contained a libel.

(2) In *Slipper v. British Broadcasting Corporation* [1990] 1 All E. R. 165 the plaintiff, a senior police officer, claimed that he was defamed in a film about his unsuccessful attempts to secure the extradition of one of the Great Train Robbers and that the BBC had caused widespread repetition of the libel through reviews in the television columns of newspapers. The Court of Appeal held that in appropriate cases the original publisher may be liable where a third party repeats the sting of the libel.

Selected Defences to Defamation

Justification (or Truth)

Key Principle: The burden of proof is on the defendant to show that the statement was true rather than on the plaintiff to prove that it was false. But it is not necessary to prove the literal truth of every word if the facts of the defamatory statement are true in substance.

Alexander v. North Eastern Railway Co. 1865
The plaintiff was charged for travelling on a train from Leeds for which his ticket was not valid and for refusing to pay the proper

fare. He was convicted and sentenced to fourteen days imprisonment in default of payment of the fine and costs. The defendant published a statement which said that the plaintiff was sentenced to three weeks' imprisonment.

HELD: Justification succeeded because the statement was not sufficiently inaccurate to defeat the defence. The defendant only has to prove "the sting of the libel". (1865) 6 B. & S. 340

COMMENTARY
(1) What constitutes a minor inaccuracy is ultimately a matter of interpretation of the facts in each case. In *Wakley v. Cooke and Healy* (1849) 4 Exch. 511, the defendant called the plaintiff a "libellous journalist" and showed evidence that he had once been successfully sued for libel. The defence failed because in the context the words meant that the plaintiff habitually libelled people.

(2) The Defamation Act 1952, section 5 provides that where two or more distinct charges are made against the plaintiff the defence will not fail by reason only that the truth of every charge is not proved. The Civil Evidence Act 1968, section 13 provides that proof of a previous conviction is conclusive evidence that a person committed the crime. Where allegations are based on criminal convictions which have become "spent", the Rehabilitation of Offenders Act 1974, section 8, provides that justification may be used as a defence except in cases where the publication has been made with malice.

Key Principle: The defendant may widen the meaning of the words relied on by the plaintiff to show that they impute a more general wrongdoing than that imputed in a particular instance.

Williams v. Reason 1988
The allegation was that the plaintiff, an amateur rugby player, had written a book for money and had thereby compromised his amateur status as a Rugby Union player.

HELD: In pleading justification the defendant was allowed to introduce evidence showing the plaintiff to have received "boot money" from a manufacturer of sports equipment was allowed. The sting of the libel was "Shamateurism" and not merely the writing of the book. [1988] 1 All E.R. 262

COMMENTARY
The defendant may only justify a meaning which the words
are reasonably capable of bearing. In *Bookbinder v. Tebbit*
[1989] 1 All E.R. 1169, a local politician was specifically
accused of squandering public money by overprinting sta-
tionery with words supporting nuclear-free zones. The
words, in the context in which they were used, were not
capable of meaning a large scale squandering of public
money and the Court of Appeal refused to allow evidence
showing a wide range of alleged instances of irresponsibility
with public money.

Fair Comment

Key Principle: Fair comment protects honest expressions of opinion based on true facts made in good faith on matters of public
interest.

London Artists Ltd v. Littler 1969
The four top performers in a play terminated their contracts
through their agents, the plaintiffs. The defendant producer was
convinced that there was a plot to stop the play. He wrote and
published a letter suggesting that the plaintiffs and the actors had
taken part in a plot to end a successful production. The trial judge
held the plea of fair comment to fail because the matter was not
one of public interest.
HELD: (CA) Although the appeal was dismissed on a different
ground (see p. 106), public interest was interpreted widely, Lord
Denning said:

"Whenever a matter is such as to affect people at large, so that
they may be legitimately interested in, or concerned at, what is
going on; or what may happen to them or to others; then it is a
matter of public interest on which everyone is entitled to make
fair comment."

The defence is available, for example, for comments made on
matters of government, public figures, literature and art. [1969]
2 Q.B. 375.

Comment and Fact

Key Principle: The statement must be a comment based on true facts but it is not necessary that all the facts upon which the comment is based should be specified in the alleged libel.

Kemsley v. Foot 1952
The defendants attacked a newspaper by publishing an article headed: "Lower than Kemsley". Kemsley, a newspaper proprietor not connected with the newspaper attacked, sued the defendants alleging that the article's heading imputed that his name was a byword for false and foul journalism.
HELD: (HL) The defence of fair comment was available. The words implied certain conduct and commented on that conduct and it was sufficiently clear that the relevant facts were the conduct of the Kemsley Press. [1952] A.C. 345

COMMENTARY
(1) The facts upon which the comments are based must be true, in *London Artists Ltd v. Littler* (see p. 105) the comment was in the public interest but the defence failed: the defendant could not prove the correctness of the underlying fact that there had been a plot between the plaintiff theatre owners and the actors. One of the questions which arose was whether the allegation of a plot was a statement of fact or comment. The court concluded that it was a fact. But what is fact and what is opinion is not always clear. In *Dakhyl v. Labouchere* [1908] 2 K.B. 325, the plaintiff described himself as a "specialist for the treatment of deafness, ear, nose and throat diseases", the House of Lords held that defendant's statement which described him as "a quack of the rankest species" might be comment rather than fact and he was entitled to raise the defence of fair comment.
(2) By the *Defamation Act 1952*, s.6 the defence of fair comment will not fail merely because the truth of every allegation of fact is not proved.

Key Principle: In deciding whether the statement is one of fact or comment the court must confine itself to the subject matter of the publication and cannot have regard to the wider context of the material.

Telnikoff v. Matusevitch 1991

The defendant had written an angry and critical letter to the *Daily Telegraph* refuting an article written by the plaintiff. The key issue was whether in determining which parts of the letter constituted allegations of fact and which were merely comment, the letter could be read alongside the offending article.

HELD: (HL) The court was confined to considering the letter itself. Readers of the letter would not necessarily have read the original article and the publication in question must be judged on its own merits. [1992] 2 A.C. 343

Fairness of the Comment

Key Principle: The defence of fair comment can be defeated by proving that a statement was made with malice which, in this instance means evil motive, spite or ill will.

Thomas v. Bradbury, Agnew & Co. Ltd 1906

A book reviewer for *Punch* had written a critical review of the plaintiff's book to which they pleaded fair comment. The reviewer's personal hostility against the plaintiff's books was evident not only from the review itself but also by his behaviour in the witness-box and elsewhere.

HELD: (CA) The defendant's malice negatived a plea of fairness. [1906] 2 K.B. 627

COMMENTARY

To be fair the defendant must have honestly believed the opinion expressed. In *Slim v. Daily Telegraph* [1968] 2 Q.B. 157, the court stated it to be irrelevant that a reasonable person would not hold such an opinion. Lord Denning said: ". . . the right of fair comment is one of the essential elements which go to make up our freedom of speech. We must ever maintain this right intact. It must not be whittled down by legal refinements."

Absolute Privilege

The following defences to defamation arise not from the content of the defamatory statement but from the circumstances of its publication or the identity of the publisher. These are *privilege* defences. *Absolute privilege* is not affected by proof of malice and a person defamed on an occasion of absolute privilege has no legal redress no matter how untrue of malicious a statement may be. Absolute privilege protects: statements in respect of anything said in parliamentary proceedings; judicial proceedings; communications made in the course of official duty by one officer of state to another and; fair and accurate newspaper and broadcast reports of judicial proceedings in the United Kingdom.

Daniels v. Griffiths 1997

The plaintiff was serving a life sentence imposed in 1993 for rape. He claimed that the defendant had defamed him by telling police that there had never been any form of relationship between them. The defendant also claimed that she was concerned for her safety should the plaintiff be released because he was fixated by her. It was submitted that publication of this statement to the police for the purposes of providing information to the Parole Board should be protected by absolute privilege on ground of public policy.

HELD: (CA) To extend the immunity attached to court proceedings to communications to the Parole Board would be unwarranted, since its proceedings were not part of the proceedings of a court of law.

COMMENTARY

In *Waple v. Surrey County Council*, *The Times*, December 29, 1997, the Court of Appeal stated that in actions for libel the courts should be slow to extend the rule about absolute privilege granted to statements made in connection with judicial or quasi-judicial proceedings.

Qualified privilege

Qualified privilege operates only to protect statements which are made without malice and it is for the judge to determine whether the occasion was privileged and whether the communucation was made with reference to the privileged occasion.

Key Principle: An occasion is privileged if the statement is made in pursuance of a legal, social or moral duty *only* if the person to whom the statement is made also has an interest or duty to receive the information.

Watt v. Longsdon 1930

The defendant, a company director, received a letter from the foreign manager of the organisation. The letter alleged that the plaintiff, who was managing director of the company abroad, was immoral and dishonest. The defendant informed the company chairman of his suspicion that the plaintiff was misbehaving with women. He also communicated the statements, which were false, to the plaintiff's wife.

HELD: (CA) The communication to the chairman was privileged because both publisher and receiver had a common interest in the affairs of the company. The publication to the plaintiff's wife was not privileged because the defendant had no social or moral duty to inform her about unsubstantiated allegations even though she might have an interest in hearing them. [1930] 1 K.B. 130

Key Principle: If the defendant honestly believed the statement to be true qualified privilege will not be lost even if the belief is arrived at from unreasoning prejudice or was irrational.

Horrocks v. Lowe 1975

The plaintiff, a Conservative Party councillor in Bolton, complained that at a council meeting the defendant, a leading Labour Party opposition member, made defamatory remarks about him. The trial judge held that the occasion was privileged but that the defendant, being in the grip of gross and unreasonable prejudice, was guilty of malice.

HELD: (HL) However prejudiced or irrational, the plaintiff's belief in the truth of what he said on that privileged occasion entitled him to succeed in his defence of privilege. [1975] A.C. 135

COMMENTARY

In *Spring v. Guardian Assurance* (1994) (see p. 74) the Court of Appeal finding that a duty of care in negligence would undermine the defence of qualified privilege, which can only be defeated on proof of malice, was overruled by the House of Lords. The majority held that the preservation of the law of defamation would not be sufficient to deny the plaintiff a remedy. It may therefore be possible to frame an action in negligent misstatement if the defamatory statement causes actual loss.

---

11. OCCUPIERS' LIABILITY

The liability of occupiers towards persons injured on their premises is governed by two statutes. The Occupiers' Liability Act 1957 is concerned with liability to lawful visitors. Liability to persons other than visitors (*e.g.* trespassers) is governed by the Occupiers' Liability Act 1984.

Occupiers' Liability Act 1957

Section 2(1) provides:

"An occupier of premises owes the same duty, the 'common duty of care', to all his visitors, except in so far as he is free to and does extend, restrict, modify or exclude his duty to any visitor or visitors by agreement or otherwise."

Occupier

Key Principle: The 1957 Act does not define "occupier" but provides that the rules of the common law shall apply. An occupier is one who has sufficient control over the premises so as to be under a duty of care towards lawful entrants: there can be more than one occupier of the same premises at any one time.

Wheat v. Lacon (E.) & Co. Ltd 1966
The defendant brewing company were owners of a pub which was run by a manager. They granted him a license to use the top floor of the premises for his private accommodation. His wife took in paying guests and one evening as it was getting dark a guest fell

down the back staircase in the private portion of the premises and was killed. The handrail on the stairs was too short and did not stretch to the bottom of the staircase and someone had removed the light bulb from the top of the stairs.

HELD: (HL) There may be two or more occupiers at any one time. Although the grant of a license to occupy had been made to the manager the defendants remained occupiers and under a duty of care. On the facts of the case the duty to the deceased had not been broken and the defendants were not liable. [1966] A.C. 522

Key Principle: **It is possible to become an occupier without taking actual physical possession of the premises.**

Harris v. Birkenhead Corporation 1976

A compulsory purchase order was made on a house and the local authority served notices of entry on the tenant and the owner. The tenant left the house and before the local authority moved in to have the property boarded up a child got in and was injured. The local authority argued that before it could be an occupier there had to be an actual or symbolic taking possession on its behalf.

HELD: (CA) The argument was rejected. Because it had the legal right to control the state of the property the local authority had become an occupier when the tenant vacated the premises. [1976] 1 W.L.R. 279

COMMENTARY

For the purposes of the Act, section 1(3) occupiers' duties apply not only to land and buildings, "premises" means any fixed or movable structure. In *Wheeler v. Copas* [1981] 3 All E.R. 405, a ladder was held to come within the definition.

Lawful Visitor

The Act brings together the previous categories of invitee and licensee into one category of visitor. Under the section 1(2) of the Act the common duty of care is owed to all lawful visitors and includes invitees, licensees and those who have a contractual right to enter. Where a person enters under a contract a term will be implied into the contract that the visitor is owed the common duty of care section 5(1). Persons who enter under a right conferred by law, whether or not they have the occupiers' express permission, enter as visitors section 2(6). In *Robson v. Hallett* [1967] 2 Q.B. 939, it was held that police officers entering without a warrant may take advantage of the generally implied license to approach a front door via the garden path. It remains important to distinguish visitors from other entrants because the duties of an occupier to other entrants is governed not by the 1958 Act but by the later 1984 Act.

Key Principle: **A person who claims to have entered a premises under an implied permission must prove that an implied license has been granted.**

Lowery v. Walker 1911

For 35 years members of the public had used a short cut across the defendant's field to a railway station. Although he had attempted to prevent this he had never taken any serious action to do so because most of the people involved were customers for his milk. The plaintiff was savaged by a dangerous horse which had been put into the field by the defendant.

HELD: (HL) The plaintiff had an implied license and was not a trespasser. [1911] A.C. 10

Key Principle: **Permission may not be implied merely because the occupier knows of the entrant's presence or has failed to take the necessary steps to prevent entry.**

Edwards v. Railway Executive 1952

Children had been accustomed to climbing through a fence dividing a recreation ground from a railway. The Railway Executive knew this and had taken steps to deter entry by repairing the fence whenever damage had been observed. The plaintiff child had got through the fence and was injured by a passing train.

HELD: (HL) The plaintiff was a trespasser and not an implied visitor. Lord Goddard observed that "repeated trespass of itself confers no license." [1952] A.C. 737

COMMENTARY

The occupier may set limits on the visitor's permission as to time, place or purpose of visit. A person who has permission only to enter a certain part of the premises has no permission to go to another part. In *The Calgarth* [1927] P. 93

Scrutton L.J. said that "When you invite a person into your house to use the stairs, you do not invite him to slide down the banisters."

Common Duty of Care

Section 2(2) of the Act provides that:

"The common duty of care is a duty to take such care as in all the circumstances of the case is reasonable to see that the visitor will be reasonably safe in using the premises for the purposes for which he is invited or permitted by the occupier to be there."

The standard of care expected under section 2(2) is the same as that in an ordinary action in negligence. In *Wheat v. Lacon* (see p. 110) Lord Denning said: "This duty is simply a particular instance of the general duty of care which each man owes his 'neighbour'". The following cases will illustrate the operation of certain aspects of the duty of care as specified in section 2(3) of the Act. Meanwhile, it should be noted that under the Act it is the visitor that must be reasonably safe and not necessarily the premises.

Children

Key Principle: Section 2(3)(a) provides that "an occupier must be prepared for children to be less careful than adults."

Glasgow Corporation v. Taylor 1922
A seven-year old child died from eating poisonous berries which he had picked from a shrub in a public park. The berries looked like cherries or large blackcurrants. It was alleged that the local authority knew of the poisonous nature of the berries but the shrub was not fenced nor was any warning of the danger given
HELD: (HL) The defendants were liable. The tempting-looking berries constituted an "allurement" to children. [1922] 1 A.C. 44

COMMENTARY
(1) In *Latham v. Johnson & Nephew* [1913] 1 K.B. 398 the court said that there is a duty not to lead children into temptation. But an object, such as a pile of stones against a wall, could not possibly constitute a trap and will not amount to an allurement.

(2) In *Jolley v. Sutton London Borough Council* [1998] 3 All
E.R. 559, a derelict boat had constituted an allurement and a
trap but these were not the causes of the accident. The
immediate cause was that the plaintiff, a 14-year-old boy
and a friend decided to repair the boat and jacked it up with
a car jack. The Court of Appeal held that, even making full
allowance for the unpredictability of children's behaviour it
was not reasonably foreseeable that the boys would work
under a propped up boat. The damage was too remote
because it occurred in an unforeseeable manner.

Key Principle: In some circumstances occupiers are entitled to
assume that parents will exercise reasonable care for their
children's safety.

Phipps v. Rochester Corporation 1955
A boy aged five and his sister aged seven walked across a large
open space which was being developed by the defendants. It was
known to the defendants that people crossed their land but they
apparently took no action. A long deep trench, which would have
been obvious to an adult, had been dug in the middle of the open
space. The plaintiff fell in and broke his leg.
HELD: The defendants were not liable. Devlin J. placed the
responsibility for small children primarily on their parents and
concluded that both the parents and the occupier must act reasonably. [1955] 1 Q.B. 450

COMMENTARY
In *Simkiss v. Rhondda Borough Council* [1983] 81 L.G.R.
460 this reasoning was followed and the plaintiff failed. A
seven-year old girl fell off a steep slope which was situated
opposite the block of flats where she lived. Her father stated
in evidence that he had not considered the slope to be
dangerous and the Court of Appeal concluded that if the
child's father did not consider the area dangerous, the defendants could not be asked to achieve a higher standard of
care.

Common Calling

Key Principle: Section 2(3)(b) of the 1957 Act provides that an occupier may expect that a person, in the exercise of his calling, will appreciate and guard against special risks ordinarily incident to it.

Roles v. Nathan 1963
Two chimney sweeps were called to clean an old coke-burning boiler which smoked badly. They were warned by an expert that the sweep-hole and inspection chamber should be sealed before the boiler was lit. They disregarded the warning and died when they were overcome with the fumes.
HELD: (CA) The occupier was not liable. His duty had been discharged by warning the sweeps of the particular risks and also, he could reasonably expect a specialist to appreciate and guard against the dangers arising from the very defect that he had been called to deal with. [1963] 1 W.L.R. 1117

COMMENTARY
Lord Denning said: "If it had been a different danger, as for instance if the stairs leading to the cellar gave way, the occupier might no doubt be responsible."

Key Principle: Skills possessed by the entrant will not automatically absolve the occupier of all liability under section 2(3)(b)

Salmon v. Seafearer Restaurants 1983
A fireman entered a fish-and-chip shop to extinguish a fire. There was an escape of gas followed by an explosion in which the fireman was injured. The defendant argued that an occupier's duty to a fireman attending a fire at his premises was limited to protecting him from special or exceptional risks over and above ordinary risks which are a necessary part of his job.
HELD: The court rejected this argument. Woolf J. took the view that although an occupier could expect a fireman attending a fire at his premises to be skilled in protecting himself against the risks of fire, an occupier could not be exempt from risks which would threaten a fireman who was exercising the normal skills of his profession. [1983] 3 All E.R. 729

COMMENTARY
The House of Lords expressly approved this approach in
Ogwo v. Taylor [1988] A.G. 431. A fireman had entered
the roof space of the defendants house to control a fire.
Although he was exercising reasonable care in using a hose
he suffered severe burns from scalding steam. The defendant
contended that no liability arose from an injury caused by
the ordinary risks involved in fire-fighting. This contention
was rejected, but, if the fireman took a foolhardy and unne-
cessary risk in fighting the fire his own conduct might break
the chain of causation.

Warning of Danger

Under section 2(4)(a) a warning of the danger may discharge
the duty of care. But the Act specifically states that a warning notice is not enough unless in all the circumstances it
enables the visitor to be reasonably safe. In *Rae v. Mars
(U.K.) Ltd* [1990] 3 E.G. 80 it was held that where an unusual
danger exists the visitor should not only be warned, but a
barrier or added notice should be placed to show the imme-
diacy of the danger.

Liability for Independent Contractors

Key Principle: Under section 2(4)(b) an occupier will not be
liable for damage caused to a visitor due to the faulty execution
of work by an independent contractor provided:

(i)   that it was reasonable to entrust the work to an indepen-
        dent contractor;

(ii)   the occupier had taken reasonable care to see that the
        contractor was competent; and

(iii)   the occupier had taken reasonable care to see that the
        work was properly done. The more technical the work the
        more reasonable it will be to entrust it to an independent
        contractor.

Haseldine v. C. A. Daw & Son Ltd 1941
The plaintiff was injured when the lift in a block of flats fell to the
bottom of its shaft. The accident happened as a result of the

negligence of a firm of independent contractors who the defendant had employed to repair the lift.

HELD: The defendant was not liable. He had discharged his duty by employing a competent firm of engineers to make periodical inspections of the lift. Having no technical skills meant that he could not be expected to check that the work had been satisfactorily done. [1941] 2 K.B. 343

COMMENTARY
This case was distinguished in *Woodward v. The Mayor of Hastings* [1945] K.B. 174, where a child at school slipped on an icy step and was injured. The step had been left in a dangerous condition by a cleaner, and even assuming that the cleaner was an independent contractor, the defendants were liable since there was no technical knowledge required to check the cleaning of a step.

Key Principle: Occupiers will not normally be expected to supervise the contractor's activities to ensure that they operate a safe system of work for the employees. Competent contractors can be presumed to have safe systems.

Ferguson v. Welsh 1987
A tender awarded by a district council for the demolition of a building stipulated that the work must not be subcontracted without the council's consent. The plaintiff was the employee of a subcontractor who had been carrying out the work without the council's consent. He suffered serious injury as a result of the subcontractor's unsafe system of work. When it was discovered that neither the main contractor nor the subcontractor were covered by insurance, he sued the local authority as occupiers of the premises.

HELD: (HL) The district council was not liable. It would not ordinarily be reasonable to expect an occupier—having engaged a contractor whom he has reasonable grounds for regarding as competent—to supervise the contractor's activities in order to ensure that he was discharging his duties to his employees to observe a safe system of work. [1987] 3 All E.R. 777

Key Principle: In certain circumstances an occupier may be liable for negligently failing to prevent deliberate injury done by one visitor to another.

Cunningham v. Reading Football Club 1991

Police officers on duty at a football match were injured by hooligans who broke off loose pieces of the concrete from the football ground and hurled them at the police.

HELD: The wrongdoing of the visitors was foreseeable and the club was liable. The concrete could easily be prised up and a similar incident had happened four months previously. *The Times*, March 22, 1991.

Acceptance of Risk

Key Principle: Section 2(5) provides that the common duty of care does not impose on an occupier any obligation in respect of risks willingly accepted as his by the visitor.

Simms v. Leigh Rugby Football Club Ltd 1969

A rugby-league player was thrown against a wall in the course of a tackle and as a result suffered injury to his leg.

HELD: The defendants were not liable. The plaintiff, a professional rugby player, had accepted the risk of playing on a rugby ground that complied with the bye-laws of the Rugby League. [1969] 2 All E.R. 923

COMMENTARY

(1) This is a specific application of the general defence of *volenti non fit injuria* (see p. 122)

(2) In *Bunker v. Charles Brand & Sons Ltd* [1969] 2 Q.B. 480 it was stated that section (5) had to be read in conjunction with section 2(4), the effect of this is that knowledge of the danger is not sufficient to establish *volenti* unless it was enough to enable the visitor to be reasonably safe.

(3) See also *Rathcliff v. McDonnell* (1998) (see p. 122)

Exclusion of Liability

Key Principle: The liability of occupiers (section 2(1) above) can be excluded "by agreement or otherwise" but the ability of business occupiers to exclude liability has been severely restricted by *Unfair Contract Terms Act 1977.* However, private occupiers, within certain limits, still have freedom to exclude liability.

Ashdown v. Samuel Williams & Sons Ltd 1957
The second defendants occupied industrial premises surrounded
by land owned by the first defendants. Access to the defendant's
land was by two roads, one of which was safe. The other road, a
short cut, could be used at the user's risk and notices to that effect
had been posted on the land. The plaintiff was taking a short cut
when she was injured by the negligent shunting of railway trucks.
HELD: (CA) The defendants, who had taken all reasonable steps
to bring to the plaintiff's attention the conditions attached to their
permission to enter, were not liable. [1957] 1 Q.B. 409

COMMENTARY
Even though this was a pre-Occupier's Liability Act 1957
decision it is still good law. In *White v. Blackmore* [1972] 2
Q.B. 651 a majority in the Court of Appeal concluded that it
was an effective defence. The plaintiff's husband was killed
at a jalopy race when a car's wheel became entangled in the
safety ropes and he was catapulted 20 feet through the air. A
notice had been posted at the entrance to the course, and at
other points about the field, absolving the defendants of all
liability arising from accidents. The deceased was held to
have entered subject to these conditions.

Contributory Negligence

The Law Reform Contributory Negligence Act 1945 applies
to an action for a breach of the common duty of care (see
p. 76). Where the visitor's failure to use reasonable care for
his/her own safety is a cause of the harm suffered the
amount of damages will be reduced in the same manner as
in an ordinary negligence action.

Liability to Entrants Other Than "Visitors"

The Occupier's Liability Act 1984

The 1984 Act, section1(1)(a) is concerned with the duty of
an occupier to "persons other than his visitors." The Act
applies to three categories of entrants:

(i)   trespassers

(ii)   persons who enter land in the exercise of rights conferred

　　　　by the National Parks and Access to the Countryside Act
　　　　1949 and

(iii)　persons lawfully exercising a private right of way.

However, in practice the most important category of entrant
to which the Act applies is trespassers. For the purposes of
section 1(3) of the 1984 Act a duty will arise if three requirements are met. First, the occupier must be aware of the
danger or have reasonable grounds to believe that it exists.
Secondly, the occupier must know or have reasonable
grounds to believe that the entrant is either in the vicinity
or may come into the vicinity of the danger concerned.
Finally, the risk is one against which, in all the circumstances
of the case, the occupier may reasonably be expected to offer
the non-visitor some protection. The duty, when it arises, is
defined by section 1(4) as the duty to take such care as is
reasonable in all the circumstances of the case to see that the
non-visitor does not suffer injury on the premises by reason
of the danger concerned.

Key Principle: The mere fact that a defendant had taken measures to stop entry onto land containing some danger does not
necessarily mean that the "reasonable grounds to believe" element
in section 1(3)(b) has been satisfied.

White v. St. Albans District City and District Council 1990
The plaintiff, a trespasser, was taking a short cut across the
defendants' fenced-off property when he fell into a trench and
was injured.
HELD: (CA) The defendants were not liable. The fact that an
occupier has taken precautions to stop people getting onto land
where there was a danger does not necessarily mean that he had
reason to believe that someone was likely to come into the vicinity
of the danger for the purposes of section 1(3)(b). *The Times,*
March 12, 1990

Key Principle: **The statutory duty owed by occupiers to non-visitors under the 1984 Act, which replaces the common law "duty of common humanity" owed to trespassers, is similar to the obligation at common law.**

British Railways Board v. Herrington 1972
The plaintiff, aged six, was badly burned when he was trespassing on the defendants land. The child had obtained access to the land through a gap in a chain link fence. The gap was used as a short cut by members of the public and the fence had been trodden down. The defendants knew that in the past children had been seen on the line, but they took no action.
HELD: (HL) Although the plaintiff was a trespasser he could recover in negligence. A trespasser is owed a lower duty of care, nevertheless an occupier does owe a duty to act humanely. [1972] A.C. 877

Key Principle: **An occupier may owe a duty to a trespasser who is engaged in committing a crime at the time of the injury.**

Revill v. Newbury 1996
In order to guard his allotment shed the defendant was sleeping in it armed with a loaded shotgun. The plaintiff, a 21-year old man, who had already committed crimes of damage to property and theft that night, tried to break into the defendant's shed. The defendant, who shot the plaintiff through a hole in the door of the shed, was sued for the resulting personal injuries.
HELD: (CA) The defendant was liable, he had used greater force than was reasonably necessary in defence of himself or his property. [1996] 1 All E.R. 291

COMMENTARY
(1) The defendant's liability for negligence, in firing the gun through the door when he was unable to see whether there was anyone on the other side, was not dependant on his status as an occupier. The plaintiff's injury, which related to the defendant's *activity* on the premises rather than the *state* of the premises itself, was governed by the common law and the 1984 Act did not apply.
(2) The defence of illegality of the plaintiff's conduct was not allowed but his damages were reduced by two thirds for contributory negligence.

Defences

Any duty in respect of risk may, by taking reasonable care in all the circumstances, be discharged by a warning section 1(5). The defence of *volenti non fit injuria* is preserved by the 1984 Act: no duty is owed by virtue of section 1(6) to any person in respect of risks willingly accepted as his/hers by that person. The 1984 Act is silent on whether the duty owed to trespassers can be excluded.

Key Principle: Volenti non fit injuria has to be considered in determining if a duty of care exists. If the trespasser willingly accepts the risk there is no duty owed by the occupier.

Rathcliff v. McDonnell and Another, 1998

The plaintiff, a nineteen-year-old student, having drunk about four pints, agreed to go swimming with two friends. At about 2.30 a.m. they climbed over the gate of a college open-air swimming pool and, although conscious of the word "Warning", the plaintiff did not read the notice by the gate. He got undressed and took a running dive into the pool either at the point where the shallow end started or at the slope from the deep to the shallow end. He hit the top of his head on the bottom, suffering tetraplegic injuries.

HELD: The Court of Appeal held that the occupiers owed no duty under section 1 of the Occupiers' Liability Act 1984. Knowing that the pool was closed for the winter, that it was dangerous to dive into water of unknown depth and that the water level of the pool was low, the plaintiff had willingly accepted the risk as his within the meaning of section 1(6). *The Times*, December 3, 1998

---

12. NUISANCE

Private Nuisance

Private nuisance, which is not the same tort as public nuisance, is commonly defined as an unreasonable interference with the use or enjoyment of land. In *Crown River Cruises*

Ltd v. Kimbleton Fireworks Ltd [1996] 2 Lloyds Rep. 533 the plaintiffs claimed in negligence, nuisance and under the principle in *Rylands v. Fletcher* for damage caused to their floating barge and a passenger vessel moored alongside it, following a fireworks display held by the defendants on the River Thames. *Kimbleton Fireworks* had argued that that the essence of nuisance was the use or enjoyment of land— not a floating barge. It was held that a permanently moored barge, occupied under a mooring licence, could sustain an action.

Although the same state of affairs may constitute both private and public nuisance, it must be noted that the rules relating to them are not identical. The central issue in the whole law of nuisance is the question of reasonableness and what constitutes unreasonable interference. In nuisance the law does not concentrate so much on the reasonableness of the defendant's *conduct* but rather on the unreasonableness of the *interference*, it seeks to strike a balance between the rights of occupiers to use their property as they choose and the rights of their neighbours not to have their use of land interfered with. In *Sedleigh-Denfield v. O'Callaghan* (below) Lord Wright said a useful test is what is reasonable according to the ordinary usage of mankind living in a particular society. As the following cases will illustrate, the approach taken by the courts to the protection of such interests is one of compromise, a "rule of give and take, live and let live": *Bamford v. Turnley* (1862) 3 B. & S. 66

Types of Actionable Interference

Key Principle: **The overflow of water onto the land of another constitutes physical damage and is actionable in nuisance.**

Sedleigh-Denfield v. O'Callaghan 1940

Without the defendants' permission—and therefore technically trespassing—the Middlesex County Council laid a pipe in a ditch on their land. The workmen involved did not place a grid near the mouth of the pipe to prevent leaves and debris blocking it. The defendants were aware of the trespass and the ditch was cleaned out twice a year on their behalf. Some years later, after a heavy rainstorm the pipe became blocked and caused flooding on the plaintiff's adjoining land.

HELD: (HL) The defendants' were liable for the nuisance because they were aware of its presence. They ought to have appreciated the risk of flooding and taken reasonable steps to abate it. [1940] A.C. 880

COMMENTARY
In *Leakey v. National Trust* [1980] Q.B. 485, a land slip was held to constitute a nuisance.

Key Principle: **Damage caused by roots of trees which encroach into adjacent land constitutes a nuisance.**

Davey v. Harrow Corporation 1958
Roots of trees which were growing on the defendant corporation's property had penetrated the land of the plaintiff's adjoining property. This encroachment caused extensive damage to the plaintiff's house.
HELD: (CA) The plaintiff was entitled to succeed, Lord Goddard said: ". . . if trees encroach, whether by branches or roots, and cause damage, an action for nuisance will lie . . ." No distinction is to be drawn between trees which may have been self-sown and trees which were deliberately planted on land. [1958] 1 Q.B. 60

Key Principle: **The emanation of smells which interfere with the plaintiff's comfort or convenience can amount to a nuisance.**

Bone v. Seal 1975
Nauseating smells had emanated from a village pig-farm for a period of 12 years. The plaintiffs did not suffer ill health but they were disgusted by the smells.
HELD: (CA) The plaintiffs succeeded. An injunction was granted and damages awarded to compensate for the loss of amenity in the enjoyment of their property. [1975] 1 All E.R. 787

COMMENTARY
(1) In *Tetley v. Chitty* (see p. 134) noise coming from a go-cart track which could be heard in the plaintiffs' houses was held to be a nuisance.
(2) In *Laws v. Florinplace* [1981] 1 All E.R. 659 a sex shop in

a residential street was held to constitute an unreasonable interference with enjoyment of property.

Unreasonable Interference—Locality

Key Principle: In assessing whether the interference amounts to an actionable nuisance the nature of the locality is taken into account. However, in cases where the interference causes physical damage to property this rule does not apply.

St. Helen's Smelting Co. v. Tipping 1865

The plaintiff purchased a very valuable estate which was within a mile and a half of a large smelting works. Fumes from a copper smelter damaged trees and crops on the plaintiff's land. The defendant contended that the whole neighbourhood was devoted to similar manufacturing purposes and that the smelting should be allowed to carry on with impunity.

HELD: (HL) The defendants were liable. The court drew a distinction between nuisances causing property damage and those causing personal discomfort. Lord Westbury highlighted that the locality rule applies only to cases of personal discomfort and does not apply where there is physical damage to the plaintiff's property. Property damage must not be inflicted wherever the defendant is carrying on the activity. (1865) 11 H.L. Cas. 642

COMMENTARY

(1) Interference which would not be permissible in one area may be in another. In *Sturges v. Bridgman* (1879) (see p. 135) Thesiger L.J. said: ". .what would be a nuisance in Belgrave Square would not necessarily be so in Bermondsey."

(2) Not every interference with enjoyment of property will amount to a nuisance. Personal discomfort is measured by reference to the standards of an ordinary person who might occupy the plaintiff's property. To be actionable the inconvenience ought to be more than fanciful it must be:

> ". . . an inconvenience materially interfering with the ordinary comfort physically of human existence, not merely according to elegant or dainty modes and habits of living, but according to plain and sober and simple notions among the English people."

per Knight-Bruce V.-C. in *Walter v. Selfe* (1851) 4 De G. & Sim. 315.

Key Principle: The granting of planning permission to facilitate
an activity on a site already used for that purpose does not carry
with it an immunity in nuisance in respect of implementation of
that planning permission.

Wheeler v. J. J. Saunders Ltd 1995

The defendants had obtained planning permission for two pig
weaning houses to facilitate the intensification of pig farming on
a site already used for that purpose. In response to the plaintiff's
claim in nuisance the defendants contended that, since they had
obtained planning permission, any smell emanating from the pigs
kept in the weaning houses could not amount to a nuisance.

HELD: (CA) The defendants were liable. Staughton L.J. stated
that, unless one was prepared to accept that any planning decision
authorised any nuisance which must inevitably flow from it, the
argument that the nuisance had been authorised by planning
permission in the instant case had to fail. *The Times,* January
3, 1995

COMMENTARY

This view was endorsed in *Hunter v. Canary Wharf Ltd* and
Hunter v. Docklands Development Corporation (1996) (not
an issue on appeal to HL, see p. 129). The Court of Appeal
rejected the submission that the powers and duties conferred
on planning authorities were such that, in granting planning
permissions, they were conferring an immunity in nuisance
on works pursuant to the permissions.

Duration

Key Principle: In determining the reasonableness of the interference the duration of the alleged nuisance will be taken into
account.

Harrison v. Southwark and Vauxhall Water Co. 1891

The defendants, in the exercise of their statutory powers, sank a
shaft into land adjoining the plaintiff's house. In the course of
carrying out the work a certain amount of noise and vibration was
created. The plaintiff brought an action in nuisance in respect of
this interference.

HELD: As the disturbance was only temporary and for a lawful
object it was not an actionable nuisance. Vaughan Williams J. said
that a man who pulls down his house for the purpose of building a
new one no doubt causes considerable inconvenience to his next

door neighbour but he is not liable in nuisance ". . . if he uses all reasonable skill and care to avoid annoyance to his neighbour." [1891] 2 Ch. 409

COMMENTARY
If the temporary interference is substantial it may amount to a nuisance. In *De Keysers Royal Hotel Ltd v. Spicer Bros Ltd* (1914) 30 T.L.R. 257, pile driving at night during temporary building works was held to be a nuisance.

Key Principle: The existence of a nuisance is usually associated with a continuing "state of affairs" but an isolated event can give rise to an action.

British Celanese v. Hunt Capacitors 1969
The defendants stored strips of foil used for making electric components on their premises. Some of the strips were blown by the wind on to an electricity power station and caused the power supply to be cut off. The plaintiffs were manufacturers of synthetic yarn which solidified when their machinery came to a halt as a result of the power cut.
HELD: A one-off event can create an actionable nuisance and the defendants were liable. [1969] 2 All E.R. 1252

COMMENTARY
The one-off event in question arose from a continuing "state of affairs" (storing the strips of metal) for which the defendants were responsible. In *S.C.M. v. Whittall* [1970] 1 W.L.R. 1017 Thesiger J. said that:

> "while there is no doubt that a single isolated escape may cause the damage that entitles a plaintiff to sue for nuisance, yet it must be proved that the nuisance arose from the condition of the defendant's land or premises or property or activities thereon that constituted a nuisance."

Sensitivity

Key Principle: **In considering what is reasonable the law does not take account of abnormal sensitivity in either persons or property.**

Robinson v. Kilvert 1889

The defendant's manufacture of paper boxes in the cellar of a building required hot and dry air and they heated the cellar accordingly. This raised the temperature on floor above and resulted in damage to the plaintiff's stock of brown paper.

HELD: The heat would not have harmed normal paper and therefore the defendant was not liable. (1889) 41 Ch. D. 88

COMMENTARY

If normal paper would have been harmed the defendant would have been liable. In *McKinnon Industries v. Walker* [1951] 3 D.L.R. 557 the plaintiff's business of growing orchids was unusually sensitive. However, the noxious fumes from the defendant's factory would have damaged non-sensitive plants and the plaintiff was able to recover the full extent of the loss, including the damage to the sensitive orchids.

Key Principle: **If the interference is due to the sensitivity of the plaintiff and is one which would not disturb ordinary healthy people, there is no redress.**

Heath v. Mayor of Brighton 1908

The plaintiff, a minister of religion, sought an injunction against the operators of a slightly noisy electricity generator. The noise, although annoying the plaintiff, did not prevent him from preaching or conducting his services and it would not have disturbed ordinary healthy people.

HELD: The injunction was not granted because the noise was not such as to distract the attention of ordinary healthy persons attending the church. (1908) 98 L.T. 718

Key Principle: Sensitivity to television reception was held (in 1965) not to be actionable in nuisance because the activity was sensitive and interference with the recreational amenity of television viewing was not a substantial interference.

Bridlington Relay Co. v. Yorkshire Electricity Board 1965
The plaintiffs operated a television relay service to provide their customers with a television signal by cable which was better than they could otherwise receive. The defendant's electricity cable interfered with the reception and affected the plaintiff's business. HELD: The plaintiff failed, according to Buckley J., because he had an unusually vulnerable business which, if it were to prosper, required an exceptional degree of immunity from interference. In addition, interference with radio and television reception was found not to be a substantial enough interference to give rise to an action in nuisance. [1965] Ch. 436

COMMENTARY
This decision would probably not be followed today. In *Nor-Video Services v. Ontario Hydro* (1978) 84 D.L.R. (3rd) 221 on similar facts the Canadian courts refused to follow it and held television reception to be a protectable interest.

Key Principle: In certain circumstances, an action for interference with television reception might be protected. However, "more is required than the mere presence of a neighbouring building to give rise to an actionable private nuisance."

Hunter v. Canary Wharf Ltd and Hunter v. Docklands Development Corporation 1997
The plaintiff and hundreds of others claimed damages for nuisance from Canary Wharf Ltd for interference, over a period of years, with reception of television broadcasts at their homes in east London. The interference was caused by the existence of the Canary Wharf Tower which is 250 metres high and over 50 metres square with stainless steel cladding and metalised windows. HELD: (HL) The erection or presence of a building in the line of sight between a television transmitter and other properties was not actionable as an interference with the use and enjoyment of land. [1997] 2 W.L.R. 684

COMMENTARY
In *Nor-Video Services v. Ontario Hydro and Bridlington Relay Ltd v. Yorkshire Electricity Board* the cause of the

interference with the television reception was an electrical power point operation. In the present case, it was the presence of the building and not any activity in the building which interfered with the television signal.

Social Utility of the Defendant's Conduct

Key Principle: In balancing the conflicting interests of neighbours the utility of the defendant's conduct is a factor, albeit a small factor, that is taken into account.

Miller v. Jackson 1977
In 1972 the plaintiff bought a house. It was built in such a place that it was inevitable that cricket balls from a cricket ground nearby would be hit into the garden. Cricket had been played on the ground since 1905 but the plaintiff contended that since the houses were built it had become a substantial interference and claimed in negligence and in nuisance.

HELD: (CA) The playing of cricket was held to constitute an unreasonable interference with the plaintiff's enjoyment of land and was therefore a nuisance. [1977] Q.B. 966

COMMENTARY
(1) Because of the pleasure derived from cricket and its social utility in keeping village communities together, Lord Denning argued that cricket playing could not be a nuisance for those living near to the ground into whose property cricket balls would be hit. However, the majority considered that the social utility of cricket could not justify a substantial interference in the plaintiff's enjoyment of their land.
(2) Note that in this case no injunction was granted to restrain the cricket. The court took the view that the utility of the club outweighed the plaintiff's interest. (See defences p. 135.)
(3) In *Adams v. Ursell* [1913] 1 Ch. 269 the utility of a fish and chip shop to local poor inhabitants could not justify its presence in a fashionable street.

Malice

Key Principle: Conduct which is motivated by malice may convert what would otherwise have been a reasonable act into an actionable nuisance.

Christie v. Davie 1893
The plaintiff, a music teacher, lived in a semi-detached house. The defendant, who lived next door, was annoyed by the music lessons and in retaliation he banged on the party-wall, beat trays, whistled and shrieked.
HELD: An injunction was granted but North J. indicated that he would have taken a different view of the situation if the defendant's acts had been "innocent". [1893] 1 Ch. 316

Key Principle: The presence of malice in the defendant's conduct in the use of their own land may tip the balance towards finding the user unreasonable.

Hollywood Silver Fox Farm Ltd v. Emmett 1936
The defendant's premises adjoined the plaintiff's silver fox farm. The vixens of these animals are very nervous during breeding-time and are likely to devour their young if disturbed. In attempting to prevent the foxes from breeding the defendant discharged guns on his own land as near as possible to the boundary of the plaintiff's land in order to scare the foxes.
HELD: Macnaghten J. considered the intention of the defendant to be relevant in nuisance and an injunction and damages were awarded. [1936] 2 K.B. 468

Who Can Sue?

Key Principle: The traditional view has been that only those who have a legal interest in the land affected can sue in private nuisance.

Malone v. Laskey 1907
Vibrations on the defendant's property caused the collapse of a cistern in the adjoining premises. The plaintiff, the wife of the occupier of the adjoining premises, suffered injury as a result.
HELD: She had no claim in private nuisance because she had

no proprietary or possessory interest in the land. [1907] 2 K.B.
141

COMMENTARY
(1) In *Khorasandjian v. Bush* [1993] 3 All E.R. 669 (see p.
5), the Court of Appeal held that the plaintiff, who lived
with her mother and had no proprietary interest in the
property, was entitled to an injunction to restrain a private
nuisance in the form telephone harassment. Dillon L.J.
said:

> "To my mind, it is ridiculous if in this present age the law is
> that the making of deliberately harassing and pestering tele-
> phone calls to a person is only actionable in the civil courts if
> the recipient of the calls happens to have the freehold or a
> leasehold proprietary interest in the premises in which he or
> she has received the calls."

(2) However, in *Hunter v. Canary Wharf* (1997) (p. 129) the
House of Lords overruled this decision and put beyond
doubt the principle that a propriety interest in land is
required to found an action in private nuisance.

Who can be Liable?

Key Principle: The creator of the nuisance may be sued and
liability extends beyond those in occupation of land themselves
and covers those who create a nuisance while on somebody else's
land.

Southport Corporation v. Esso Petroleum 1956
The defendant's oil tanker ran aground and there was a danger
that she might break up with the probable loss of the ship and
the loss of the lives of her crew. In order to prevent this the
master decided to lighten the ship and 400 tons of oil were
discharged into the sea. The river estuary was polluted and the
plaintiff corporation alleged that the deposit of oil on the fore-
shore gave rise to three causes of action: trespass, nuisance and
negligence.
HELD: (HL) A nuisance, which need not emanate from private
land, had been committed. [1956] A.C. 218

COMMENTARY
The defence of necessity succeeded in this case and the defendants were absolved of liability. Where life and limb are at risk any necessary damage to property will be justified.

Key Principle: Occupiers who become aware of the existence of a nuisance arising out of a natural condition on their land are bound to take positive action.

Goldman v. Hargrave 1967
A redgum tree, 100 feet high, on the defendant's land was struck by lightning and caught fire. The defendant caused the land around the burning tree to be cleared and the tree was then cut down. He did not extinguish the fire after doing this in the belief that the fire would eventually burn itself out. However, it kept smouldering and subsequently the wind increased and the fire spread to the plaintiff's land.
HELD: (PC) The occupier was liable for failing to take adequate precautions to extinguish the fire in the face of foreseeable risk. [1967] 1 A.C. 645

COMMENTARY
(1) The Privy Council applied the rule in *Sedleigh-Denfield v. O'Callaghan* (see p. 123) where the occupiers were held liable for the *nuisance* created by a *trespasser*. In that case the occupiers had made use of the pipe laid by the trespasser to drain water from their land and were therefore found to have both adopted and continued the nuisance.
(2) In *Leakey v. National Trust* [1980] Q.B. 485 the Court of Appeal extended the principle in Goldman to include nuisances caused by the *natural condition of the land itself.* Because of its geological structure, land owned by the defendants was prone to subsidence which caused land slips onto the plaintiff's property. Although they had been warned of the possibility of a substantial earth slip, the defendants refused to do anything about it and merely gave the plaintiff permission to abate the nuisance at his own expense. The defendants were liable for failing to take appropriate action when they knew of the risk.

Key Principle: The general rule is that a landlord who has leased premises is not liable for nuisances arising from them except where the landlord granted the lease for the purpose which constitutes the nuisance.

Tetley v. Chitty 1986

Residents in Rochester complained of noise from a go-cart track which could be heard in their houses. The Medway Borough Council had granted planning permission for the go-cart track on its land and had granted a lease to a go-cart club. The local authority, having leased the land was no longer in occupation of it.
HELD: The local authority was liable: excessive noise was a very predictable consequence of the use for which the land had been let. [1986] 1 All E.R. 663

Key Principle: A landlord who has an obligation to repair or who reserves the right to enter and repair may be liable.

Wringe v. Cohen 1940

Because of want of repair, a wall to the defendant's premises collapsed and damaged the plaintiff's shop. The house was let to a weekly tenant but the defendant was liable to keep the premises in repair. He did not know that the wall was in a dangerous condition and that it had, as a consequence of this, become a nuisance.
HELD: (CA) The defendant was liable and the court stated:

> "If, owing to want of repair, premises on a highway become dangerous and, therefore, a nuisance a passer-by or an adjoining owner suffers damage by their collapse, the occupier, or owner if he has undertaken the duty of repair, is answerable whether he knew or ought to have known of the danger or not." [1940] 1 K.B. 229

COMMENTARY

See also public nuisance (see p. 137).

Selected Defences

Twenty Years Prescription

Key Principle: The continuation of a nuisance for twenty years will, by prescription, legalise a private nuisance (but not a public one). However, it is not sufficient for the defendant to show that the activity has been carried on for twenty years, the interference must have amounted to an actionable nuisance for period of twenty years.

Sturges v. Bridgman 1879
The defendant's premises adjoined those of the plaintiff, a medical practitioner. For over 20 years the noise and vibrations from the defendants business as a confectioner had not interfered with the plaintiff's use of land. The plaintiff then built a consulting room in the garden and complained of the noise. Prescription was pleaded as a defence.
HELD: The defence failed because time ran from when the new building was erected and the nuisance had only commenced from that date. (1879) 11 Ch.D. 852

Statutory Authority

Key Principle: If a statute authorises the defendant's activity the defendant will not be liable for interferences that are an inevitable result of that activity.

Allen v. Gulf Oil Refining 1981
A private Act of Parliament authorised Gulf Oil to acquire land by compulsory purchase for the building of an oil refinery in order to facilitate the importation and refinement of crude oil and petroleum products. However, the Act contained no express authority for the use and operation of the refinery once it had been built. After the refinery had been in operation the plaintiff, living in the vicinity, alleged that it caused a nuisance by smell, noise and vibration.
HELD: (HL) Gulf Oil were entitled to statutory immunity in respect of any nuisance which they were able to prove was an inevitable result of constructing the refinery which conformed to the intention of Parliament. Lord Diplock commented that:

"Parliament can hardly be supposed to have intended the refinery to be nothing more than a visual adornment to the landscape in an area of natural beauty". [1981] A.C. 101

COMMENTARY
It should be noted that the granting of planning permission
by a local authority (under its own statutory powers) does
not give immunity to an action of nuisance in respect of that
permission. See *Wheeler v. J.J. Saunders Ltd* (1995).

Ineffective Defences

Key Principle: It is no defence that the plaintiff came to the
nuisance by occupying the land adjoining it.

Bliss v. Hall 1838
The plaintiff occupied a property adjoining the premises of the
defendant candle-maker. The plaintiff alleged nuisance in the
emission of smells and noxious vapours which resulted from the
candle-making process. The defendant argued that the business
has been carried on in the same premises for three years before the
plaintiff came to the adjoining property.
HELD: This would not defeat the plaintiff's claim. The justification for the rule is that it would be unreasonable to expect someone not to purchase land because a neighbour was abusing their
rights. (1838) 4 Bing. N.C. 183

COMMENTARY
(1) This rule has recently been confirmed by the Court of
Appeal in *Miller v. Jackson* (see p. 130) where Lane L.J.
stated:

> "It is no answer to a claim in nuisance for the defendant to
> show that the plaintiff brought the trouble on his own head by
> building or coming to live in a house so close to the defendant's
> premises that he would be inevitably be affected by the defen-
> dant's activities where no one had been affected previously."

However, note Lord Denning's dissenting view on this point.
(2) It is also no defence that the defendant's activity is a
useful one (see *Adams v. Ursell*) nor is it a valid defence to
allege and prove that the nuisance resulted from the combined acts of different persons, even though the actions of
each of them would not, taken individually, amount to a
nuisance.

Remedies

Injunction

Key Principle: An injunction is the primary remedy in an action for nuisance and its objective is to force the defendant to cease the nuisance or limit it to certain times.

Kennaway v. Thompson 1981
The plaintiff had built a house by a man-made lake and was disturbed by water-skiing and speed-boat racing which the defendant club was beginning to organise. The defendants were held liable for the nuisance created by the noise but they argued that an injunction should not be granted on the ground that there was a public interest in permitting the watersports to continue. The trial judge had taken into account the public's interest in having sports facilities available to it and, exercising his discretion, awarded damages instead of an injunction.
HELD: (CA) The plaintiff was granted an injunction and the traditional view was reasserted: that if there is an actionable nuisance the plaintiff should win an injunction. [1981] Q.B. 88

COMMENTARY
The court was not prepared to give priority to the public interest and the decision in *Miller v. Jackson* (see p. 130) was criticised. However, the injunction granted to the plaintiff was formulated in terms which did amount to a compromise which was obviously influenced by public interest. Motor-boat racing was permitted to continue on the lake subject to the injunction restricting the number and extent of racing activities in each year and the noise level of boats using the lake at other times.
(2) An injunction is one of three remedies available to a plaintiff in nuisance: the other two being damages and a limited form of self-help known as "abatement".

Public Nuisance

Key Principle: A public nuisance is an act or omission which materially affects the reasonable comfort and convenience of life of a class of Her Majesty's subjects (*per* Romer L.J.)

Attorney-General v. P.Y.A. Quarries Ltd 1957

The defendants used a system of blasting which created dust noise and vibrations and also caused stones and splinters to project from their quarry into the neighbourhood. There were two highways and about thirty houses close to the quarry and the defendants contended that there was at most a private and not a public nuisance.

HELD: (CA) Any nuisance is "public" which materially affects a class of her Majesty's subjects. The number of persons to constitute a class of the public is a question of fact in every case. [1957] 2 Q.B. 169

Key Principle: **In order to succeed in an action for public nuisance a plaintiff must suffer "particular damage" over and above the damage sustained by the public generally.**

Tate & Lyle Food and Distribution Ltd v. G.L.C. 1983

Ferry terminals constructed by the defendants in the River Thames caused excessive silting. This disrupted the plaintiff's business by obstructing access to their jetty and they had to spend large sums on dredging operations. Their claim in private nuisance was dismissed because: (1) the jetty itself was unaffected and (2) they had no private rights of property in the river bed.

HELD: (HL) It was their public right to use the river which had been damaged and their claim lay in public nuisance alone. The expenditure incurred by the plaintiffs on dredging constituted particular damage over and above the ordinary inconvenience suffered by the public at large, and was therefore recoverable. [1983] 2 A.C. 509

COMMENTARY

(1) The rule that a plaintiff who does not have possession or a proprietary interest in land cannot sue in private nuisance has been confirmed by the House of Lords in *Hunter* (see p. 129).

(2) A danger arising from a premises adjoining the highway constitutes a public nuisance: *Wringe v. Cohen* (see p. 134).

13. THE RULE IN *RYLANDS V. FLETCHER*

Key Principle:

". . . the person who for his own purposes brings on his lands and collects and keeps there anything likely to do mischief if it escapes, must keep it in at his peril, and, if he does not do so, is prima facie answerable for all the damage which is the natural consequence of its escape." *per* Blackburn J., (1866) L.R. 1 Ex. 265

Rylands v. Fletcher 1868

The defendant mill owners employed independent contractors, who were apparently competent, to build a reservoir on their land to provide water for their mill. Beneath the site there were some disused mine shafts and passages which, unknown to the defendants, were connected to the plaintiff's mine. The contractors negligently omitted to block the old shafts and when the reservoir was filled the water burst through them and flooded the plaintiff's mine.

HELD: (HL) The House of Lords affirmed the decision of the Court of Exchequer Chamber that the defendants were liable but Lord Cairns rested his decision on the ground that the defendant had made a "non-natural use" of his land. (1868) L.R. 3 H.L. 330

COMMENTARY

(1) There is overlap between *Rylands v. Fletcher* and nuisance but the rule in *Rylands v. Fletcher* is concerned with escapes from the land rather than interference with land.

(2) The defendant must be in control of the dangerous thing. However, it is not necessary for the defendant to have a proprietary interest in the land from which the dangerous thing escapes. In *Rigby v. Chief Constable of Northamptonshire* [1985] 1 W.L.R. 1242, when the police discharged a CS gas canister from the highway, Taylor J. commented that he could:

"see no difference in principle between allowing a man-eating tiger to escape from your land on to that of another and allowing it to escape from the back of your wagon parked on the highway."

Non-Natural User

Key Principle: Lord Cairns' requirement in *Rylands v. Fletcher* of "non-natural use" has been established as part of the rule. The courts have interpreted natural to mean something which is ordinary and usual and non-natural use is equated with extraordinary use or activity.

Rickards v. Lothian 1913
By a malicious act an unknown third party blocked a domestic water system. The water overflowed and caused damage to the plaintiff's premises on the floor below.
HELD: (PC) There was no liability under *Rylands v. Fletcher* because the supply of water via normal domestic installations was a natural use of land. [1913] A.C. 263

COMMENTARY
(1) Lord Moulton defined non-natural use as "some special use bringing with it increased danger to others." In *Read v. Lyons* (see p. 141) it was argued that operating a munitions factory in wartime is a natural use of land. Lord Porter said that in deciding the question of non-natural user:

> "all the circumstances of time and practice of mankind must be taken into consideration so that what may be regarded as dangerous or non-natural may vary according to the circumstances."

For example, in *Musgrove v. Pandelis* [1919] 2 K.B. 43, it was held that keeping a car in a garage with a full tank of petrol was a non-natural use.
(2) The word "dangerous" is not interpreted literally and there is no requirement that the thing which escapes must be dangerous. Plainly dangerous things such as explosives and gas come within *Rylands v. Fletcher* but the rule has also applied to a "chair-o-plane" in a fairground, *Hale v. Jennings Bros* (1938) (see p. 143), and, in *Attorney-General v. Corke* [1933] Ch. 89, it even applied to gypsies!

Key Principle: There seems to be a similarity between the way in which the concept of non-natural use is generally applied by the courts and the idea of unreasonable risk in negligence.

Mason v. Levy Auto Parts of England Ltd 1967

The defendants stored on their land large quantities of combustible materials. When they inexplicably caught fire the plaintiff's ornamental hedge was burned.

HELD: The defendants were liable. [1967] 2 Q.B. 530

COMMENTARY

(1) The kinds of factors which led the judge to find there had been a non-natural user were the kinds of factor which would also have to be considered in an action for negligence.
(2) In *British Celanese v. Hunt* (see p. 127) when the plaintiffs alleged that the metal strips had escaped and caused the power failure, the liability did not arise under *Rylands v. Fletcher* on the ground that the manufacture of electrical components on an industrial estate was not a non-natural user of land, as that was the very purpose for which the land was designed. But in *Cambridge Water Co. v. Eastern Counties Leather plc* (1994) (see p. 142) the House of Lords held that storage of substantial quantities of chemicals on industrial premises is an almost classical case of non-natural use, even in an industrial estate.

Key Principle: The rule applies to things which the defendant deliberately accumulates on the land: it does not apply to things which are naturally on the land.

Giles v. Walker 1890

When the occupier ploughed up forest land a large crop of thistles sprang up and the seeds were blown onto the neighbouring land.
HELD: The defendant was not liable because the danger was not caused by the defendant's intervention but was the product of natural forces. (1890) 24 Q.B.D. 656

COMMENTARY

Following *Leakey v. National Trust* there may now be liability in nuisance or negligence in circumstances such as these.

Escape

Key Principle: **For the rule to apply there must be an "escape" from the defendant's premises.**

Read v. J. Lyons & Co. Ltd 1947

The plaintiff was employed as an inspector in the defendant's munitions factory. In the course of her employment she was injured by the explosion of a shell that was being manufactured on the premises. There was no allegation of negligence on the part of the employers.

HELD: (HL) As there had been no "escape" of the thing that inflicted the injury *Rylands v. Fletcher* was inapplicable, and in the absence of negligence the plaintiff's claim failed. [1947] A.C. 156

Damage

Key Principle: **Foreseeability of damage of the relevant type should now be regarded as a prerequisite of liability in damages under the rule in *Rylands v. Fletcher*.**

Cambridge Water Co. v. Eastern Counties Leather plc 1994

The defendants, an old established leather manufacturer, used a chemical solvent PCE in their tanning process. PCE evaporates quickly in the air but is not readily soluble in water. In the course of the process, before a change of method in 1976, continual small spillages had gradually built up a pool of PCE under their premises. The solvent seeped into the soil below and contaminated the aquifer from which the plaintiffs drew their water. At first instance the claim in *Rylands v. Fletcher* was dismissed because it was held that there was no non-natural user of the land. The nuisance action failed because at the time the contamination was taking place it was not foreseen that the quantities of the chemical would accumulate or that if it did, there would be any significant damage.

HELD: (HL) The claims in negligence and nuisance failed for lack of foreseeability. The action in *Rylands v. Fletcher* also failed because the defendants had not known, and could not reasonably have foreseen, that the seepage would cause the pollution. [1994] 2 W.L.R. 53

Key Principle: There is dispute about whether a plaintiff must have an interest in land in order to maintain an action under *Rylands v. Fletcher.* However, a non-occupier has succeeded in respect of damage to property.

Halsey v. Esso Petroleum Co. Ltd 1961

The defendants operated an oil-distributing depot near to the plaintiff's house in a partly residential area in Fulham. The depot operated day and night and the plaintiff complained of the following:

(i)   acid smuts from a boiler in the depot which damaged the plaintiff's washing;

(ii)   the same smuts which caused damage to his car standing on the road outside;

(iii) a smell escaping from the depot which was nauseating but caused no damage to health;

(iv)   noise from lorries in the depot; and

(v)   noise from tankers on the road outside leaving and arriving throughout the day and night.

HELD: There was liability under (i) for nuisance and *Rylands v. Fletcher* and under (ii) there was liability under *Rylands v. Fletcher* and in public nuisance. [1961] 1 W.L.R. 683

COMMENTARY

(1) There was also liability for (i) and (iv) in private nuisance. Liability was based on private nuisance or in the alternative in public nuisance by virtue of the defendant's use of the highway. The character of the neighbourhood was also relevant to the question of nuisance by smell and by noise. This case provides a useful illustration of the application of public and private nuisance and the rule in *Rylands v. Fletcher.*

(2) In *Read v. Lyons* (see p. 141) it was said *obiter* that the plaintiff must be an occupier in order to maintain an action under the rule in *Rylands v. Fletcher* and in *Weller & Co. v. Foot & Mouth Disease Research Institute* it was held that the plaintiffs could not succeed under the rule because they did not have an interest in land affected by the escape.

Key Principle: The position with regard to recovery for personal injuries under *Rylands v. Fletcher* is not clear, but an occupier of land was held to be entitled to damages under *Rylands v. Fletcher.*

Hale v. Jennings Bros 1938
A chair became detached from a "chair-o-plane" in a fairground and a stallholder suffered personal injuries as a result of the escape.
HELD: Recovery for the plaintiff's personal injury was allowed. [1938] 1 All E.R. 579. In *Read v. Lyons* (see p. 141) doubts were raised about whether the rule in *Rylands v. Fletcher* could be used in a claim for personal injury. In *Hunter v. Canary Wharf* it was held that personal injuries are not, *per se*, recoverable.

Defences

Liability under *Rylands v. Fletcher* is strict but it is not absolute. There will be no liability where the plaintiff has consented to the accumulation, unless the defendant had been negligent in causing the escape, nor will the defendant be liable where the damage is caused by the plaintiff's own act. Statutory authority is a defence (as in *Allen v. Gulf Oil*) and the defence of necessity is also available.

Act of a Stranger

Perry v. Kendricks Transport 1956
The defendants parked a coach in their vehicle park which was bordered by some waste land. The petrol tank had been drained but an unknown person had removed the cap. A boy of about ten threw a lighted match into the petrol tank which exploded causing the child plaintiff, who was crossing the wasteland at the time, to be badly burned.
HELD: (CA) The defendants were not liable as the explosion was caused by the act of a stranger over whom they had no control. [1956] 1 All E.R. 154

COMMENTARY
This principle applied in *Rickards v. Lothian* (see p. 140).

Act of God

Key Principle: The defendant is not liable where the escape is caused by natural forces in circumstances "which no human foresight can provide against, and of which human prudence is not bound to recognise the possibility."

Nichols v. Marsland 1876
The defendant had artificial ornamental lakes on his land which were formed by damming up a natural stream. Following a thunderstorm there was an unprecedented rainfall which caused the banks of the ornamental lake to burst and destroy bridges on the plaintiff's land.
HELD: The defendant was not liable. There was found to be no negligence because the flooding was caused by an act of God. (1876) 2 Ex. D.I.

COMMENTARY
On very similar facts, in *Greenock Corporation v. Caledonian Railway* [1917] A.C. 556 the application of this defence was criticised by the House of Lords. The rainfall was found not to be an act of God and the Corporation were held to be under a duty to make sure that owners or occupiers on a lower ground level are as secure against injury as they would have been had nature not been interfered with.

INDEX